D0772441

Even More Unofficial Recipes from Minecraft, Game of Thrones, Harry Potter, Twin Peaks, and More!

THE GEEKY CHEF STRIKES BACK!

Cassandra Reeder, the Geeky Chef

Race Point PUBLISHING

Dedicated to my family, who have always embraced and supported me in all my strange ways.

Brimming with creative inspiration, how-to projects, and useful information to enrich your everyday life, Quarto Knows is a favorite destination for those pursuing their interests and passions. Visit our site and dig deeper with our books into your area of interest: Quarto Creates, Quarto Cooks, Quarto Homes, Quarto Lives, Quarto Drives, Quarto Explores, Quarto Gifts, or Quarto Kids.

First published in 2017 by Race Point Publishing, an imprint of The Quarto Group, 142 West 36th Street, 4th Floor, New York, NY 10018, USA
T (212) 779-4972 F (212) 779-6058 www.QuartoKnows.com

Race Point titles are also available at discount for retail, wholesale, promotional, and bulk purchase. For details, contact the Special Sales Manager by email at specialsales@quarto.com or by mail at The Quarto Group, Attn: Special Sales Manager, 401 Second Avenue North, Suite 310, Minneapolis, MN 55401, USA.

10 9 8 7 6 5 4 3 2 1

ISBN: 978-1-63106-293-3

Library of Congress Cataloging-in-Publication Data

Names: Reeder, Cassandra, author.
Title: The Geeky Chef strikes back! : even more unofficial recipes from
    Minecraft, Game of Thrones, Harry Potter, Twin Peaks, and more! /
    Cassandra Reeder, the Geeky Chef.
Description: New York : Race Point Publishing, [2017] | Includes index.
Identifiers: LCCN 2017002344 | ISBN 9781631062933 (hardcover)
Subjects: LCSH: Cooking. | Food in motion pictures. | Food on television. |
    Food in popular culture. | LCGFT: Literary cookbooks.
Classification: LCC TX714 .R437 2017 | DDC 394.1/2--dc23
LC record available at https://lccn.loc.gov/2017002344

Editorial Director: Jeannine Dillon
Project Editor: Jason Chappell
Managing Editor: Erin Canning
Photographer: Bill Milne
Food Stylist: Kristy Hollidge
Photography Production Manager: Noah Rosenbaum
Photography Production Assistant: Micaela Pereira-Castillo
Illustrations: Denis Caron
Interior Design: Jacqui Caulton

Printed in China

CONTENTS

INTRODUCTION

This is still hard for me to believe, but, here I am . . . older, possibly wiser (but probably not), and much like the Empire, I'm striking back! You wouldn't think that there are so many people who like making and eating "fictional" food. Even with the giant geek pride boom we're all lucky enough to exist in, it's still a niche within a niche. And yet, here we are! There's enough of us that some crazy people let me make another cookbook.

"Striking back" is the official unofficial theme of this cookbook. With so many geeky classics getting reboots, remakes, adaptations, prequels, sequels, reimaginings, and whatever else you can possibly think of, I found myself stumbling on a lot of recipes that may be making a comeback. There's a lot to be excited and nostalgic about . . . Excited to be nostalgic? If there's not a word for that already, someone should make that word.

Those of you who are familiar with my previous cookbook, or my blog, will probably already know that things get a little weird. Weird is just what happens when you're trying to create sometimes reality-defying fictional food. We're boldly going where no cook has gone before, and I have my own Prime Directive, and General Orders 2 and 3, to help me navigate that. Here they are:

1 I must try to do the fans and the media creators justice by making the recipes as accurate as possible.

2 I must try my best to keep things simple and avoid overly complicated methods and overly rare and/or expensive ingredients.

3 I must try to make the end product taste good. Or, if it's not necessarily supposed to taste good, I must try to at least make it edible.

Thankfully, I'm more Starfleet than Jedi, so "try" is acceptable. It's not always easy or even possible to balance these goals, and attempting to balance them equally can make the recipe suffer, but I do my best. I try.

So, thank you to the readers for being supportive of this endeavor. That's everyone who has followed the blog and everyone who bought, read, borrowed, or shared the first cookbook, too. Especially those of you who were kind enough to tweet, post, and pin about it. I never dreamed that my blog would become one cookbook, let alone two, and you are to thank for that. Or blame, depending on your opinion of this cookbook. Also, while I'm doing thank-yous, a big thanks to the creators of the works referenced in this book. I have nothing but love, respect, and adoration for you. Maybe a little obsession, too, if we're being honest.

But seriously, what are you still doing here? Does anybody actually read these introductions? I guess if anybody does, it's probably us geeks. But, still, it's time to move on. Go forth and cook!

BASIC PREP RECIPES

PREPARE TO PIE

THE YELLOW CAKE IS *NOT A LIE*

ALL YOUR SOUP BASE ARE BELONG TO US

I FIND YOUR LACK OF SIMPLE SYRUP DISTURBING

THE SPICES MUST FLOW

LIVE LONG AND MAKE IT VULCAN

You know, I've been doing this fictional food stuff for almost nine years, and something I have noticed is that a lot of fictional foods are desserts, soups, or alcoholic beverages. What's up with that? It probably speaks to the inner psyche of the human mind or something.

To simplify things, I'm going to go ahead and put some reoccurring prep recipes here. You can also feel free to use premade versions of these, or your own recipes. I'll also add a few vegan substitute suggestions for all the Vulcans out there.

PREPARE TO PIE

Pie dough is intimidating and, honestly, sometimes buying a premade one from the store is totally worth it. However, if you are willing to spend the time and energy to make a superior homemade crust, this recipe will do the trick.

Single Crust
1¼ cups (155 g) all-purpose flour
1 teaspoon granulated sugar
Generous pinch salt
½ cup (1 stick, or 120 g) unsalted butter, chilled
3 tablespoons ice water

Makes dough for 1 single-crust pie.

Double Crust
2½ cups (310 g) all-purpose flour
2 teaspoons granulated sugar
¾ teaspoons salt
1 cup (2 sticks, or 240 g) unsalted butter, chilled
6 tablespoons ice water

Makes dough for 1 double-crust pie.

1 Mix the flour, sugar, and salt in a food processor. Slice the butter into the processor and pulse everything until it forms crumbs. Blend in enough ice water to create moist clumps, but not so it is all stuck together.

2 Gather the dough into a ball with your hands. If you're making double crust, divide the dough in half and form into 2 balls. Flatten into disc(s), wrap in plastic wrap and chill for at least 2 hours.

THE YELLOW CAKE IS *NOT* A LIE

Or, it doesn't have to be. You can be enjoying some cake with your companion cube in about 40 minutes. With some modifications, you can use the yellow cake recipe as the base for many cakes. It's pretty magical.

1 cup (2 sticks, or 240 g) unsalted
  butter, softened
1½ cups (300 g) granulated sugar
2 eggs, separated
2 teaspoons vanilla extract
2 cups (250 g) cake flour
1 tablespoon baking powder
1 teaspoon baking soda
1 teaspoon salt
1 cup (235 ml) buttermilk

1 Preheat oven to 325°F (170°C).

2 In a large bowl, cream together the butter and sugar.

3 Add in the egg yolks and the vanilla, mixing until fully incorporated. Set aside.

4 In a separate bowl, combine the flour, baking powder, baking soda, and salt.

5 Gradually sprinkle the dry ingredients into the wet ingredients and stir, alternating with the buttermilk.

6 Mix until the batter is fluffy, but be careful not to overmix.

7 In a separate bowl, beat the egg whites until foamy and thick.

8 Very gently fold the egg whites into the batter and mix until incorporated. Again, do not overmix.

9 Transfer to two 9-inch (23 cm) cake pans, ramekins, or two muffin/cupcake tins.

10 Bake for 30–35 minutes for the two 9-inch (23 cm) cake pans, 20–25 minutes for cupcakes or ramekins, or until a toothpick inserted in the center of a cake comes out clean.

ALL YOUR SOUP BASE ARE BELONG TO US

People get intimidated by soups, but don't worry, you're not on the way to destruction. Soup is one of the easiest things in the world to make, but there is a lot of room for error. In fact, most of the time, errors just become happy accidents. Soups can include pretty much anything you can dream of, but it all starts with a great base, and this base works for most soups.

2 tablespoons olive oil or unsalted butter
1 large or 2 medium white onions, chopped
1 teaspoon salt
2 celery stalks with leaves, chopped
1 teaspoon black pepper

1   In a soup pot, warm the olive oil or butter over a medium-high heat.

2   Once the oil is hot, add the onions and sprinkle with the salt. Stir the onions until they begin to turn translucent, 3–4 minutes.

3   Add the celery to the onion, and stir.

4   Add the black pepper and continue cooking for another 5–6 minutes, stirring once every minute.

I FIND YOUR LACK OF SIMPLE SYRUP DISTURBING

Okay, not my best pun. But, everyone who likes making drinks and cocktails should have some simple syrup in their arsenal, right next to the lightsabers. It's an easy way to sweeten up any beverage without changing the flavor or adding crunchy bits of undissolved sugar to an otherwise perfect drink. The best thing about it is that you can easily add all sorts of ingredients to make flavored syrups.

1 cup (235 ml) water
1 cup (200 g) sugar

1 Add the water and sugar to a pot and bring to a boil.

2 While the mixture boils, stir until the sugar is completely dissolved.

3 Remove from heat and let cool to room temperature, then transfer to a sealable container and store in the fridge. The simple syrup will thicken as it cools.

THE SPICES MUST FLOW

I like to use a lot of herbs and spices. If a recipe calls for two cloves of garlic, I put in about seven. Because of this, I am somewhat reluctant to add measurements for seasoning and spice. Just think of the seasoning amounts as suggestions, and follow your heart and your taste buds.

I'm including two of my go-to seasoning blends that I use in much of my cooking and baking, and which will appear in many of these recipes. You may think that mixing a spice blend is just making things unnecessarily complicated, but premixing spice and seasoning blends actually saves you a ton of time in the long run. Instead of having to individually dole out each spice, you will have it all ready to go in just one bottle.

These are a couple of basics to start you off; I highly recommend experimenting with your own seasoning blends as they're definitely one of the most useful things to have in the kitchen. You'll be amazed at the depth of flavor you can develop when you start mixing and matching your own spice blends. Bonus: You'll feel like an alchemist or a wizard with all the bottles and jars of stuff.

All-Purpose Sweet Spice Blend (a.k.a. Spice Mélange)

4 parts ground cinnamon
1 part ground allspice
1 part ground nutmeg
1 part ground cloves
1 part ground ginger

All-Purpose Savory Seasoning Blend

3 parts garlic powder
3 parts onion powder
2 parts dried parsley
1 part sea salt
1 part ground black pepper

LIVE LONG AND
MAKE IT VULCAN

For all the vegan geeks out there, here are a few ways you can make the baking recipes (and maybe some of the others) vegan.

 VEGAN-FRIENDLY INGREDIENT SWAPS

1 egg = ¼ cup (60 g) applesauce

Butter = 1:1 coconut oil

Milk = 1:1 any non-dairy milk

Buttermilk = 1:1 any non-dairy milk + 1 teaspoon lemon juice, let sit for 5 minutes

Heavy cream = 1:1 coconut milk, fat layer only

NON-ALCOHOLIC BEVERAGES

The Lord of the Rings: **ENT DRAUGHT**

Fallout: **NUKA COLA QUANTUM**

ASOIAF/Game of Thrones: **MILK OF THE POPPY**

Hook: **POE-POE**

Harry Potter: **PUMPKIN JUICE**

Star Trek: **RAKTAJINO**

ENT DRAUGHT

INSPIRED BY **THE LORD OF THE RINGS**

This beverage makes its first appearance in the second book of *The Lord of the Rings* trilogy, *The Two Towers*. As fans will know, the Ents were the ancient tree-people of Middle-earth, dwelling in Fangorn Forest. Merry and Pippin spend a lot of time in the Fangorn Forest after escaping Saruman's clutches, and there they make friends with Treebeard, the eldest of the Ents. During their time in Treebeard's "house," Merry and Pippin are given the drink of the Ents. The draught gives the Hobbits the feeling of being refreshed from the tips of their toes up to the ends of the hair on their heads, and makes Merry and Pippin grow quite a few inches taller than average Hobbit size.

The flavor of the drink is supposed to be light, as the drink is described as being like water but has a taste that reminds the Hobbits of the smell of wood from a distance carried by a cool breeze . . . or something like that. For this I used plant-based ingredients with bright earthy/leafy flavors and sweetened the drink with tree sap (maple syrup). Making this invigorating beverage is so quick and simple, you'll be done long before Treebeard can say "Ent Draught."

SERVES 1

10 mint leaves
1 tablespoon pure maple syrup
1 teaspoon lemon juice
Drop almond extract
1 cup (235 ml) lightly brewed
   green tea, chilled

1 In a serving glass, muddle the mint leaves in the maple syrup using a muddler or a wooden spoon.

2 Add the lemon juice and almond extract to the muddled mint.

3 Pour the green tea into the glass and stir to combine.

 KITCHEN NERD NOTES

To muddle mint leaves, gently press them against the bottom of the glass with your muddler or wooden spoon, while twisting your wrist for 10–15 seconds. Doing this for too long will cause the leaves to turn bitter, so don't overdo it.

NUKA COLA QUANTUM

INSPIRED BY **FALLOUT**

Fallout is Bethesda's RPG that takes place in a post-apocalyptic United States. In the alternate reality, Nuka Cola was invented in 2044 and quickly became the most popular soft drink in the world. It's supposed to contain the essence of seventeen different fruits, which gives it its unique and irresistible flavor. In addition to a super delicious and nutritious "mild radioactive strontium isotope," Nuka Cola's second version, Nuka Cola Quantum, contains an eighteenth fruit essence: pomegranate.

It was a bit of a puzzle to figure out how to make a recipe for a glowing radioactive soda with entirely artificial flavoring. Luckily, I like me some puzzles. Hawaiian Punch and Sunny D don't contain anything natural and have a mixture of fruit-like flavors, so I thought these would work pretty well for the base. I made sure to include some pomegranate syrup to make it uniquely Quantum, and the rest is pretty much self-explanatory. Prepare to increase your action points by twenty, and radiation levels by ten!

SERVES 1–2

¼ cup (60 ml) Hawaiian Punch
  (Berry Blue, or a mix of Berry Blue
  and Aloha Morning)
¼ cup (60 ml) Blue Raspberry Sunny D
½ tablespoon pomegranate syrup
  or pomegranate molasses
½ tablespoon vanilla syrup
Caffeine additive (optional), use as
  package directs
¾ cup (175 ml) soda water (or tonic
  water, but it will taste bitter)

Supplies
Old-fashioned soda bottle (optional)
Scotch tape (optional)
Nuka Cola Quantum label (optional)
Small LED light (optional)

1 In a pitcher, stir all ingredients except soda water together.

2 Add soda water (or tonic water, which will make the beverage glow under a blacklight) to mixture and stir.

3 Pour into the old-fashioned soda bottle, or other serving cup of your choice.

4 Tape your printed label to the bottle.

5 To make the soda "glow" tape the small LED light to the bottom of the bottle with the lighted side facing up into the bottle.

MILK OF THE POPPY

INSPIRED BY **ASOIAF/GAME OF THRONES**

Weirdly, this is one of the recipes I get the most requests for, and I've been avoiding it because, well . . . you guys know this is a drug, right? I know it sounds like a fun, soothing beverage but the leading theory is that it's supposed to be laudanum, which is a tincture made from opium, which is made from a certain type of poppy. That's why everyone in the series is less than enthusiastic to drink it, because even though they've just had their face sliced in half, it makes coherent thought difficult, and that's assuming you don't slip into a mini-coma for a few days. You've got to keep your wits about you when you play the game of thrones.

However, I'm happy to make a "lite" version. There are a few ingredients which have a similar—although considerably less powerful—effect. Warm milk is a soothing, natural sedative. Turmeric is a very effective natural painkiller, among many other things. Cinnamon and ginger not only taste great, they also have anti-inflammatory properties. And, even though the honey is mostly there to make this elixir more palatable, it does have some antibiotic properties. I don't recommend this drink for severe injuries, like being gored by a boar, but it will ease milder aches and pains and help you sleep.

SERVES 1–2

2 cups (475 ml) milk
1 teaspoon vanilla extract
2 teaspoon turmeric powder
½ teaspoon ground cinnamon
1–2 round slices peeled fresh ginger
Pinch black pepper
Honey, to taste

1   Pour the milk into a saucepan and set over medium heat. Add the vanilla, turmeric, cinnamon, ginger, and pepper. Stir well as the milk begins to simmer.

2   Let simmer for a minute or two, being mindful that the milk doesn't overheat.

3   Turn off the heat and cover the pan, then leave to infuse for 5–10 minutes.

4   When ready to drink, strain the milk into serving glasses, then stir in the honey.

POE-POE

INSPIRED BY **HOOK**

Most of us '90s kids have a soft spot in their heart for *Hook*, and I especially wanted to include this film in this book after the passing of Robin Williams, a fellow geek and A+ human being. One of the most memorable scenes in it was when Peter, after a long day of being tortured by adolescents, finally sits down to enjoy supper, only to learn that the Lost Boys eat imaginary food instead of real food. Peter hasn't really recovered his imagination by this point, so he watches enviously as the Lost Boys merrily chow down on their make-believe grub. That is until he gets into a very creative insult fight with Rufio and playfully slings some of the imaginary food at him. Suddenly, Peter rediscovers his imagination and can finally see the food. Obviously, an epic food fight ensues . . . because epic food fights are an inevitability in any '90s kids' film.

The imaginary smorgasbord in this scene seems to be comprised primarily of colorful whipped cream with some ham hocks and a giant cheese wheel thrown in for fun. However, one Neverfood that is mentioned by name and is briefly shown is Poe-Poe. In the script for *Hook* the food is called Papaw, which is another word for papaya, but in the film, the captions read "Poe-Poe" and it's depicted as a creamy, frothy drink that leaves a milk mustache on Peter's face when he takes a sip. My take on this frothy Neverdrink will take you back to your childhood, with hints of candy, cake, and bubblegum. *Bangarang.*

SERVES 2

2 cups (475 ml) whole milk
2 scoops orange sherbet
½ strawberry papaya, peeled,
    seeded, and cut into rough chunks
½ banana
½ teaspoon ground cinnamon
½ cup (60 g) box cake mix
Rainbow sprinkles
Whipped cream, to serve

1 Throw all the ingredients except the sprinkles and whipped cream into the blender, then blend for about a minute.

2 Add a small fistful of sprinkles and blend again for a second or two.

3 Pour into serving glasses, top with whipped cream and more rainbow sprinkles.

PUMPKIN JUICE

INSPIRED BY **HARRY POTTER**

The fantastic fictional foods in the Harry Potter books, much like the series itself, have captured the imaginations of geeks worldwide. I wasn't sure I would ever have the opportunity to write a second cookbook, so I included a lot of Harry Potter recipes in the first *Geeky Chef* volume. However, I did save one very important drink for this volume: pumpkin juice.

Pumpkin juice does seem to be the equivalent of our beloved Muggle orange juice. Witches and wizards mostly drink it with breakfast but it can be served with any meal or even enjoyed on its own. Like orange juice, it packs a punch, nutritionally speaking, being rich in fiber, antioxidants, vitamins, and minerals. It will keep you sharp and vibrant for your Potions Final and properly hydrated for a Quidditch match. You can even use it to slip your friend some liquid confidence, whether that means alcohol or Felix Felicis to you. Wizards can presumably use a spell to extract the juice from the pumpkin, but Muggles will either need a juicer (recommended) or a blender and strainer.

SERVES 2–4

1 small sugar pumpkin, peeled with
  pulp removed
1 apple, cored, peeled, and sliced
2 carrots, peeled and diced
1-inch (2.5 cm) slice peeled ginger
1 tablespoon ground cinnamon,
  or to taste
1 teaspoon vanilla extract
2 tablespoons Simple Syrup
  (page 11), or to taste

With a juicer:

1 Dice the pumpkin into small chunks.

2 Add the pumpkin, apple, carrots, and ginger to the juicer.

3 Juice the produce into your serving cup.

4 Combine the cinnamon, vanilla, and Simple Syrup, then stir that into the juice and serve!

With a blender and strainer:

1 Preheat the oven to 350°F (180°C).

2 Cut the pumpkin in half using a serrated knife.

3 Put the pumpkin halves into a clean roasting pan. Cover the pan with foil and roast for about 90 minutes or until the flesh of the pumpkin is soft and juicy but not burnt. Once cooked, the pan will have juice at the bottom, so save that and set it aside.

4   Take some of the pumpkin flesh and wrap it in some cheesecloth–you will probably have to do this a little at a time. Over a large bowl, squeeze the flesh through the cheesecloth so that the juice goes into the bowl. Get as much juice as you can–you should get about a half a quart or more from the whole pumpkin. I also recommend saving the leftover pumpkin pulp as it works great in baked goods and smoothies.

5   When you have as much juice as you're going to get from the pumpkin, combine it and the other ingredients in a blender and blend. You may want to use half the ginger, though. It will be frothy, but don't worry, it will eventually settle. Add ice to serve right away or set in the fridge for an hour or so until cool.

🍴 **KITCHEN NERD NOTES** 🍴

Warning: The juice, when obtained via the blender/strainer method, does not keep long. It tends to solidify into a gelatin-like texture after 24 hours. It can still be used for a brilliant pumpkin milkshake, though!

RAKTAJINO

INSPIRED BY STAR TREK

Raktajino is Klingon coffee. While Raktajino is sometimes enjoyed in other *Star Trek* series, it's no secret that every character in *Deep Space Nine* is hopelessly addicted to it. The first step to recovery is admitting you have a problem, DS9 crew. Honestly, I would bet that the word "Raktajino" is said more often in *Deep Space Nine* than the words "Deep Space Nine" in tandem. They may as well have named the series *Star Trek: Raktajino*.

There are no specifics about how exactly this Klingon coffee differs from Earth coffee, but we can guess that it's probably about twice as strong as a standard human coffee. After all, it's made for Klingons, who are about twice as strong as a standard human. For this recipe I combined the method of Vietnamese coffee with the spices in Moroccan-style coffees.

SERVES 1

2 tablespoons sweetened
  condensed milk
3 tablespoons ground
  (medium-coarse) medium-dark
  roast coffee with chicory
Pinch ground cardamom
Pinch ground black pepper
Pinch ground nutmeg
Pinch ground ginger
Pinch ground clove
½ cup plus 4 teaspoons
  (140 ml) boiling filtered water
1 Vietnamese coffee filter*

1 Add the sweetened condensed milk to a mug.

2 Add the coffee grounds to the base of the coffee press, then add the spices on top of the grounds. Wet these with the 4 teaspoons (20 ml) hot water.

3 Screw the press on tight, making sure the coffee is well-packed down. If you don't have the kind that screws, don't worry. Place the filter on top of the mug.

4 Pour the remaining boiling water into the coffee press and cover with the lid. Wait for the coffee to drip into the cup until all the water is gone.

5 Remove the filter, stir the coffee into the milk and enjoy!

* These can be purchased cheaply at any
  Asian grocery store or on online.

ALCOHOLIC BEVERAGES

Doctor Who: **BANANA DAIQUIRI**

Twin Peaks: **BLACK YUKON SUCKER PUNCH**

Fallout: **DIRTY WASTELANDER**

Dark Souls: **ESTUS**

Star Wars: **JAWA JUICE**

Star Trek: **BLOODWINE**

BANANA DAIQUIRI

INSPIRED BY **DOCTOR WHO**

Doctor Who fans in the UK, you guys would not believe the number of requests I get to make recipes for Jammie Dodgers and Jelly Babies. Attention all *Doctor Who* fans outside the UK, this is a public service announcement: this is not a test, Jammie Dodgers and Jelly Babies are real! They're a bit difficult to find outside the UK, but you can purchase them online and have them shipped. You're welcome!

Alright, now that's sorted, what better way to enjoy your new giant hoard of Jammie Dodgers and Jelly Babies than to wash it all down with a nice Banana Daiquiri? In the Season 2 episode "The Girl in the Fireplace," the Tenth Doctor, after partying hard with Madame de Pompadour, shows up fashionably late to save Rose and Mickey from dismemberment at the hands of clockwork robots. While doing so, the Doctor revels in the night's activities and claims to have invented the banana daiquiri a few centuries too early. So, here's what a banana daiquiri would be if you Frenched it up a bit and added Madame de Pompadour's favorite food: champagne. I tried to use only ingredients that would be available in Le Potager du Roi of Versailles in eighteenth-century France. . . . Well, aside from the banana, which, of course, you should always bring with you to a party.

SERVES 2

½ cup (140 g) crushed ice
½ cup (120 ml) water
2 shots rum
2 frozen bananas
2 teaspoons lemon juice
1 tablespoon Simple Syrup
  (page 11)
1 cup (235 ml) champagne,
  chilled

1 Combine all the ingredients except the champagne in a blender, or use your sonic screwdriver to blend it up. It'll be very thick at this point.

2 Pour the contents of the blender into 2 serving cups.

3 Top with champagne and stir.

BLACK YUKON SUCKER PUNCH

INSPIRED BY **TWIN PEAKS**

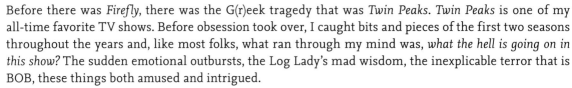

Before there was *Firefly*, there was the G(r)eek tragedy that was *Twin Peaks*. *Twin Peaks* is one of my all-time favorite TV shows. Before obsession took over, I caught bits and pieces of the first two seasons throughout the years and, like most folks, what ran through my mind was, *what the hell is going on in this show?* The sudden emotional outbursts, the Log Lady's mad wisdom, the inexplicable terror that is BOB, these things both amused and intrigued.

When people think about *Twin Peaks* food, they probably think about black coffee, jelly donuts, and that heavenly cherry pie over at the RR Diner. Don't worry, we'll get to that pie (page 118), but first this mysterious fictional cocktail deserves some attention. The Black Yukon Sucker Punch appeared in the episode "The Orchid's Curse." While Judge Sternwood is deciding whether the incapacitated Leo Johnson should be tried for his multitude of crimes, he invites Agent Cooper and Sheriff Truman over to the bar and orders up three Black Yukon Sucker Punches. This recipe uses clues from the scene (the sound of a blender, the coffee maker) to make this unusual-looking beverage. I don't know where these clues will lead us, but I have a feeling it will be a place both wonderful and strange.

SERVES 2–3

Black Liquid

2 cups (475 ml) cold brew coffee, chilled
1 shot blackberry liqueur
1 shot Yukon Jack whiskey (or any other whiskey you have)

Blue Foam

1 cup egg whites (8 eggs, or 243 g) from pasteurized eggs
½ teaspoon cream of tartar or 1 teaspoon lemon juice, freshly squeezed
1 shot blue curaçao

1 Stir the coffee, blackberry liqueur, and whiskey together and pour into 3 Collins glasses. Set aside.

2 In a small mixing bowl, use an immersion blender to blend the egg whites and cream of tartar or lemon juice until stiff peaks form. Then add the blue curaçao to the foam and blend just until the color is fully incorporated.

3 Using a ladle, transfer the foam on top of the black liquid into the Collins glasses.

4 Drink up, but be careful—these will sneak up on you!

DIRTY WASTELANDER

INSPIRED BY **FALLOUT**

The *Fallout* series of games is set in a post-apocalyptic world after a nuclear war. Like all Bethesda games, *Fallout* is so immersive that it's easy to lose yourself exploring. There's so much freedom, you can do big important things, like save people, or you can just wander around scavenging for bottle caps and bug meat.

Since the setting is an atompunk wasteland, most of the food is processed, irradiated, and, frankly, not very appetizing. Luckily for us, the cooking system got a very nice revamp in the fourth installment, and there were slightly more appealing recipes for consumables introduced. One of these is the Dirty Wastelander, a cocktail consisting of mutfruit, Nuka Cola, and whiskey. The mutfruit has the appearance of a blackberry/blueberry hybrid, both of which pair excellently with whiskey and cola.

SERVES 1–2

5 blackberries
8 blueberries
1 teaspoon Simple Syrup (page 11)
1 teaspoon lemon juice
Ice cubes
2 shots whiskey
1¼ cups (300 ml) cola

1   In a serving glass, muddle the blackberries, blueberries, simple syrup, and lemon juice using a muddler or a wooden spoon.

2   Add the ice cubes to the glass.

3   Pour the whiskey into the glass, top with the cola and give the drink a stir before serving.

> **KITCHEN NERD NOTES**
>
> To muddle the berries, gently press them against the bottom of the glass with your muddler or wooden spoon, while twisting your wrist for ten to fifteen seconds. Do this until most of the berries' flesh is crushed and you have released some juice.

ESTUS

INSPIRED BY **DARK SOULS**

While modern game makers focus on creating games that are intuitive and painless, *Dark Souls*, well . . . it takes a different approach. This game is notorious for its punishing difficulty. The challenges and battles are brutal, and only the most tenacious of gamers can stomach them. But even if you can't stomach *Dark Souls*, you can definitely stomach this tasty beverage based on the game's primary consumable, the Estus Flask.

Estus is the primary healing item in the game, and is therefore the player's best friend. The taste of Estus is not described but it looks pretty much like liquid sun/fire. When you look around the Internet for what *Dark Souls* fans think Estus might taste like, the answers vary from "like Sunny Delight" to "like molten lava" to–my personal favorite–"as grossly incandescent as the sun." I can't say what molten lava or, um, the sun, tastes like but, keeping these various responses in mind, I made an amalgamation of the citrus and fire responses that seemed to be common. The result is a drink that burns, yet refreshes. While battling certain death at every turn, keep this drink close at hand.

SERVES 1–2

2 shots Fireball Cinnamon Whiskey
1 cup (235 ml) orange juice
Pinch cayenne pepper (optional)
Handful ice
1 cup (235 ml) ginger beer
½ blood orange, cut in half
1 glass bottle or decanter,
  for serving

1 In a blender, blend all ingredients except the ginger beer and blood orange.

2 Pour the mixture into serving glasses.

3 Top with the ginger beer.

4 Squeeze the blood orange over the top and serve.

JAWA JUICE

INSPIRED BY **STAR WARS**

Everyone in *Star Wars* is usually too busy saving the galaxy or Force-choking their subordinates to sit down for some refreshments. However, if you look hard enough (read: really, really hard) there is some food and drink to be found in the beloved *Star Wars* films. Jawa Juice was mentioned in *Episode II: Attack of the Clones*, when it is offered to Obi-Wan Kenobi by the waitress droid in Dex's Diner. Obi-Wan and Dex himself enjoy the beverage while discussing the poisoned dart that took out Padmé's would-be assassin.

There's not much information about the drink in the film, but in the *Stars Wars* companion book, *Star Wars: Absolutely Everything You Need to Know*, there are some details to be gleaned. The drink, also called Ardees, is thankfully not actually made from Jawas but from fermented grains and Bantha hides. Which is great, because making a drink out of the little guys did seem a bit harsh. The taste of this is described as "bitter." In the original script for the film, the drink is also described as "steaming" and is served in mugs. Based on this information, it can be supposed that Jawa Juice is a warm alcoholic beverage. My take on this drink is a semi-traditional mulled beer, which has both the fermented grains (beer) and the, er, "protein" aspect covered with a tempered egg yolk to add a bit of creaminess. Trust me, it's not as weird as it sounds.

SERVES 1–2

2 cups (475 ml) ale or beer (non-alcoholic beer can be used)
Peel of 1 small orange
2 round slices fresh peeled ginger
1 teaspoon ground nutmeg
2 cinnamon sticks
4 whole cloves
1 pasteurized egg yolk
1 tablespoon granulated sugar
Simple Syrup (page 11), to taste

1. Add the beer, orange peel, ginger, and spices to a small saucepan and warm over medium-low heat.

2. In a small bowl or cup, add the egg yolk and sugar and whisk them together until the color is lightened and the consistency becomes frothy.

3. Temper the yolk/sugar mixture by very slowly adding a small amount (about a tablespoon at a time) of the hot beer and whisking it in. This will prevent the yolk from cooking.

4. Add the tempered yolk mixture slowly to the warm beer and continue to heat for 5 minutes.

5. Add Simple Syrup to taste.

6. Pour the beverage into serving glasses through a strainer.

BLOODWINE

INSPIRED BY STAR TREK

Klingons are one of the major races in the *Star Trek* universe, being featured heavily in every series since the very first one. Originally depicted as bloodthirsty and aggressive antagonists to the Federation, the characterization of Klingons—while definitely still battle-oriented—evolved to depict a culture based on honor and spirituality, similar to that of the Vikings. In addition to enjoying poetry and meditation, Klingons have a lot of pride in their very, er, *distinctive* cuisine.

Whether bloodwine is actually made from blood is still debated amongst *Trek* fans. In the official *Star Trek* cookbook, which is "narrated" by Neelix, it does claim that bloodwine is made from actual blood fermented with sugar. However, some *Trek* fans knowledgeable in the art of winemaking have insisted that it's unlikely that the results of this would be appealing, even to Klingons. But, hey, if you want to try that out, it's your *Hegh'bat*. Despite what the official cookbook says, I am going to go ahead and move forward under the assumption that, much like our own human "sangria," the name isn't literal. After all, Neelix is from the Delta Quadrant and he's not infallible. Remember that one time he somehow endangered the entire ship with cheese? What a *PetaQ*. Anyway, this version is made with red wine, prune juice (for Warf), cherries, salt, and orange liqueur. *IwlIj jachjaj!*

SERVES 3–4

2 cups (475 ml) cheap red wine,
   room temperature
1 cup (225 g) Bing and/or Hudson
   cherries, pitted
2 shots triple sec
½ cup (120 ml) prune juice
Splash orange bitters
Simple Syrup (page 11), to taste
2 pinches sea salt

1   Add all the ingredients to a blender.

2   Blend on high until completely smooth.

3   Serve in mugs.

APPETIZERS, SNACKS, AND SIDES

CHOCOLATE-FROSTED SUGAR BOMBS

INSPIRED BY **CALVIN AND HOBBES**

Calvin and Hobbes was a newspaper comic, created by Bill Watterson, that ran from 1985 to 1995. It followed a rambunctious and imaginative child, Calvin, and his best friend, a stuffed toy Tiger named Hobbes. Calvin is, like so many of us, much more comfortable dealing with aliens and talking tigers than with chores and homework.

When Calvin and Hobbes aren't exploring the many uses of corrugated cardboard boxes, they are most likely eating Chocolate-Frosted Sugar Bombs. Well, Calvin is anyway. The cereal is supposed to have a "rich, fudgy taste" and contains both caffeine and high volumes of sugar. You can eat them by themselves or add some milk and watch the white liquid turn brown!

SERVES 4–6

5 cups (150 g) Cocoa Puffs cereal
  or similar
1½ cups (260 g) semi-sweet
  chocolate chips
¼ cup (½ stick, or 60 g) unsalted
  butter
1 tablespoon instant coffee
1 teaspoon vanilla extract
1½ cups (185 g) confectioner's sugar

1 Put the cereal into a large mixing bowl and set aside.

2 In a large microwaveable bowl, microwave the chocolate chips and butter on high for about a minute until melted, then stir in the instant coffee.

3 Microwave for about 30 seconds more, until mixture is completely smooth when stirred. Then stir in the vanilla.

4 Pour this chocolate mixture over the cereal, stirring until all the puffs are evenly coated. Pour everything into a large (1–2 gallon, or 4.5–9 L) resealable plastic bag.

5 Add the confectioner's sugar to the bag, seal it and shake until each piece is well coated. Spread the mixture out evenly on a piece of wax paper to cool. Once cooled, store in an airtight container in the refrigerator.

EZTLITL STUFFED MUSHROOMS

INSPIRED BY **GUILD WARS 2**

I gave *World of Warcraft* a lot of love in the first cookbook, so I thought it would be a good idea to spread some of that love to other MMOs in this cookbook. *World of Warcraft* has been a long-standing champ of the MMO genre, but *Guild Wars 2*, with its beautiful graphics and emphasis on exploration, has given the MMO giant a run for its money. This game has really pushed the boundaries of what an MMO can be. The tough part about doing any MMO recipe is just picking which food to do. Especially when it comes to *Guild Wars 2*, which, as players know, has an array of mouthwatering consumables.

So, why Eztlitl Stuffed Mushrooms? Well—full disclosure—I needed more appetizer recipes. But also, don't they sound tasty? And who doesn't love stuffed mushrooms? Always a crowd pleaser. In the game these contain mushrooms (obviously), Eztlitl stuffing (bread, thyme, rosemary, shallot), and cheese. There's really not a lot of additional ingredients needed to make this combination amazing in real life. Enjoy!

SERVES 6–8

28 large white mushrooms
⅔ cup (160 ml) extra-virgin olive oil, divided
1 shallot, minced
2 garlic cloves, peeled and minced
Salt and black pepper, to taste
1 cup (50 g) fresh breadcrumbs
½ cup (50 g) Parmesan/Romano blend, grated, plus more for topping

1 Preheat the oven to 400°F (200°C).

2 Stem the mushrooms and set the caps aside. Chop the stems very small, almost so they're minced.

3 Heat 2 tablespoons of the olive oil in a pan, add the shallot, garlic, and chopped stems. Season with salt and pepper. Sauté over medium heat for 15 minutes, or until stems are browned and juicy. Be careful not to burn the garlic.

4 Stir the chopped stems and garlic with the breadcrumbs, cheese, thyme, rosemary, and 2 more tablespoons of olive oil in a medium bowl to blend. Stir in the seasonings.

1 tablespoon fresh thyme, chopped

½ tablespoon fresh rosemary, chopped

1 tablespoon Savory Seasoning Blend (page 12)

5 Grease the baking sheet with about 1 tablespoon of the olive oil, to evenly coat.

6 Spoon the filling into the mushroom cavities and arrange them on the baking sheet, filling side up.

7 Drizzle the remaining olive oil over the filling of each mushroom, then top with the extra cheese—make them as cheesy as you like! Bake until the mushrooms are tender and the filling is heated through and golden on top, about 30 minutes. Serve hot!

FLAMING FIRE FLAKES

INSPIRED BY **AVATAR: THE LAST AIRBENDER**

The *Avatar* series is known for having a terrific sense of humor, great animation, lovable characters, and a totally unique world. In the world of *Avatar*, some characters are gifted with the ability to manipulate or "bend" one of the four elements: earth, air, fire, and water—the Avatar being the only person who can bend all four elements. The four elements play a huge part in the world of *Avatar*, not only in bending, but in the culture of the people. The elemental powers of each of the four nations influence everything, including the food.

These little guys are the go-to snack food of the Fire Nation. They're served at plays, festivals, and other celebrations. Like many Fire Nation dishes, they pack quite a bit of heat. When Sokka first eats these, he immediately tries to scrape them off his tongue. Although later he requests that Aang bring him back the snack while watching the play about themselves on Ember Island. You can bring them along with you on the go, or you can just stress-eat them at home like Mai. Firebend your mouth!

SERVES 3–5

2 cups (60 g) rice flakes, flattened
  rice, or poha
1 tablespoon garlic chili oil
1 tablespoon olive oil
1 tablespoon toasted sesame seeds
1 teaspoon smoked paprika
Cayenne pepper, to taste
Savory Seasoning Blend (page 12),
  to taste
Salt and black pepper, to taste
2 teaspoons confectioner's sugar

1 Dry roast the rice flakes. In a hot pan or wok, turn the heat to high and add the rice flakes. Keep moving the flakes around until they become crispy and start to curl, but be careful not to let them burn. Toasting them this way usually only takes a couple of minutes. Once done, remove from the heat and set aside temporarily.

2 In the same pan, add the chili and olive oils and heat to medium-high.

3 Once the oil is hot, add back the rice flakes along with the sesame seeds and seasonings. Stir and fry for 3–5 minutes, then stir in the confectioner's sugar until thoroughly incorporated.

4 Let cool to a little above room temperature, then serve.

OTIK'S SPICED POTATOES

INSPIRED BY **DRAGONLANCE**

Dragonlance began as a gaming module for *Dungeons and Dragons*, created by Tracy and Laura Hickman. It was submitted to TSR, the publishers of *Dungeons and Dragons*, and was well received because it was heavily focused on dragons, and the gaming modules at the time were perhaps a little more Dungeons than Dragons. Many series of novels have been created based on the module. There was even an animated movie based on the first book, but, despite its impressive cast, we do not speak of it.

The first *Dragonlance* trilogy, the Chronicles series, by Tracy Hickman and Margaret Weis, is beloved. In the Chronicles series there is an inn called the Inn of the Last Home, run by a portly man named Otik. Otik's specialty dish is spiced potatoes, which are famous far and wide. It's never specifically mentioned what the potatoes are spiced with, only that they are spiced and fried. Works for me! Enjoy with a nice pint of ale.

SERVES 2–4

½ cup (1 stick, or 120 g) unsalted
  butter
1 dried red chili pepper
1 pound (450 g) fingerling potatoes,
  cut in half lengthwise
1 tablespoon Savory Seasoning
  Blend (page 12)
1 teaspoon paprika
½ teaspoon turmeric
½ teaspoon ground cumin

1 In a large skillet, heat the butter until it starts to bubble.

2 Add the dried chili and move it around the pan, then let it infuse for about a minute.

3 Add the potatoes, then sprinkle on all the spices. Use a wooden spoon or a spatula to toss the potatoes around and make sure they are well coated in the butter and spices. At this point, remove the red chili.

4 Cook on high heat for about 5 minutes or until the potatoes are slightly browned at the edges.

5 Lower the heat and cover the pan. Cook, covered, until the potatoes are fork tender.

6 Uncover the pan and increase the heat to dry off any remaining moisture. The potatoes should be crispy on the outside and soft on the inside.

7 Taste and adjust seasoning if desired. Serve hot!

PIZZA GYOZA

INSPIRED BY TEENAGE MUTANT NINJA TURTLES

Pizza has been an important part of *TMNT* from the very beginning. Any fan knows that the heroes in half shells, like most people with functioning taste buds, have a very passionate love for pizza. As an '80s baby, I grew up watching the original *TMNT* TV series. My personal favorite episode revolved around killer pizza monsters that hatched out of mutant meatballs, which Shredder planted on April O'Neil's pizza. It was totally tubular, dudes.

Since then, the turtles have had quite a few makeovers. Pizza Gyoza made its first appearance in the 2012 episode "Never Say Xever," when the turtles rescue Mr. Murakami, the blind owner of a local noodle house, from the Purple Dragons. In thanks, Murakami-san asks if he can prepare them a meal based on their favorite food. This seemingly unholy union is a bodacious fusion of pizza, the ubiquitous favorite food of the American teen, and traditional Japanese pot stickers, the snack of choice in Japan. Watch out, they're eye-poppingly tasty. *Booyakasha!* Or *Cowabunga!* if you were born before 1995.

SERVES 3–5

½ cup (110 g) tomato sauce
1 tablespoon grated Parmesan
1 teaspoon dried oregano
5–6 fresh basil leaves, chiffonade
Savory Seasoning Blend (page 12),
  to taste
20 (about ½ package) gyoza
  wrappers, thawed
10 ounces (300 g) mozzarella
  cheese, shredded
10 ounces (300 g) pepperoni,
  chopped small
2 cloves garlic, roasted and minced
2 tablespoons vegetable oil, for frying
Marinara sauce, for dipping

1 In a small bowl, mix together the tomato sauce, Parmesan, oregano, basil, and seasoning. You can also add any other Italian seasonings you like to the sauce.

2 Prep your gyoza station. You will need a clean surface, preferably wood as the dough is less apt to stick to it. Have a small bowl of water and a clean towel nearby, and line a baking sheet with parchment paper ready to place the finished gyoza on.

3 Take one gyoza wrapper and lay it on the clean surface. Spread about 1 teaspoon of the tomato sauce in the center of the gyoza, leaving plenty of room in the outside of the circle. The sauce should only take up about half the diameter of the gyoza skin.

4 Take a pinch of mozzarella cheese and sprinkle on top of the pizza sauce. Do the same with the chopped pepperoni.

5 Wet your fingers in the water and lightly moisten the edges of the gyoza wrapper, then dry your fingers on the towel. Fold the dumpling over and press the moistened inner edges together to form a half circle. Some people may want to get fancy and do pleats, but it's not necessary. Place the sealed dumpling on the lined baking sheet.

6 Repeat steps 3–5 until all the gyoza skins are gone.

7 Heat some oil in a skillet over medium-high heat. Fry the gyoza filling side down until the bottom is nice and browned but not burnt—usually just a few minutes.

8 Turn the heat to medium-low and add about ½ cup (120 ml) of water to the pan. Immediately cover with a lid to steam for 10–15 minutes.

9 Serve with chopsticks and a little bowl of marinara sauce for dipping.

⚔ KITCHEN NERD NOTES ⚔

To chiffonade the basil, stack the leaves together and roll them into a cigarette shape. Use a sharp knife to slice the rolled up leaves lengthwise, to get thin strips.

SPECIAL BELL PEPPERS AND BEEF

INSPIRED BY **COWBOY BEBOP**

As the first anime to be broadcast on Cartoon Network's Adult Swim, *Cowboy Bebop* was, for many in the West, the gateway drug into adult anime. Everything—from the music, to the action, to the characters—was stylish and cool. This series inspired my friends and me to take some of our first (incredibly bad) attempts at cosplay. It involved BB guns and rolled-up printer paper "cigarettes." Fortunately, no yellow shorts.

As far as food, it's not all self-heating ramen and Ganymede Sea Rats. Very early in the first episode of the series, Jet tells Spike he is preparing "special" beef and bell peppers. Unfortunately, it turns out that they don't actually have the funds for beef, so the meal is really just stir-fried green bell peppers and what looks like mushrooms, and probably not the kind that make you see talking frogs. Spike has . . . an emotional moment. If you've collected some good bounties lately, you can easily upgrade this dish by adding some sliced flank steak. See you, Space Cowboy . . .

SERVES 2–4

1–2 tablespoons cooking oil, for frying
8 ounce (225 g) flank steak, thinly sliced (optional)
3 cloves garlic, minced
1½ cups (150 g) shiitake mushrooms, cleaned and sliced
2 green bell peppers, seeded and cut into long, thin slices
3 tablespoons low-sodium soy sauce
2 tablespoons rice vinegar
2 teaspoons grated peeled fresh ginger
Red chili oil, to taste
2 green onions, diagonally sliced
Sesame seeds, for topping

1 Heat the cooking oil in a large non-stick skillet over medium-high heat.

2 If you're using the steak, add it to the skillet and cook for 2–3 minutes, searing on one side. If you're not using steak, proceed to step 3.

3 Add the garlic, mushrooms, and bell peppers to the skillet, and cook for 2–3 minutes, stirring constantly.

4 Remove the vegetables and beef, if using, from the pan.

5 Add the soy sauce, vinegar, ginger, and chili oil to the pan and bring to a boil for 1 minute or until the sauce thickens slightly.

6 Add back the vegetables and beef, if using, to the hot pan, along with the scallions. Toss everything to coat it in the sauce, then sprinkle with sesame seeds and serve.

TASTEE WHEAT

INSPIRED BY **THE MATRIX**

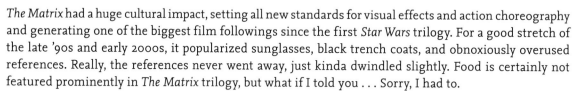

The Matrix had a huge cultural impact, setting all new standards for visual effects and action choreography and generating one of the biggest film followings since the first *Star Wars* trilogy. For a good stretch of the late '90s and early 2000s, it popularized sunglasses, black trench coats, and obnoxiously overused references. Really, the references never went away, just kinda dwindled slightly. Food is certainly not featured prominently in *The Matrix* trilogy, but what if I told you . . . Sorry, I had to.

It's not the most appetizing fictional food ever, but there *is* a fictional food in *The Matrix*—Tastee Wheat. While Neo and the rest of the crew are eating their gruel, a.k.a. "bowls of snot," Mouse comments that the gruel reminds him of "Tastee Wheat" from inside the Matrix, and that everything may or may not taste like chicken because their only context is an illusionary world. It's not specified exactly what Tastee Wheat is, but one can surmise that it's a sort of hot wheat cereal. While you're eating this surprisingly satisfying porridge, you should try to remember that there is no spoon . . .

SERVES 1–3

2 cups (475 ml) water
Pinch salt
½ cup (100 g) bulgur
1 tablespoon whole wheat flour
½ cup (120 ml) whole milk
1 teaspoon Sweet Spice Blend
  (page 12)
1 teaspoon vanilla extract
Brown sugar, for topping (optional)
Butter, for topping (optional)

1 Pour the water into a pan, season with salt and bring to a boil. Once boiling, stir in the bulgur, then cover and cook on low heat for 15 minutes.

2 Meanwhile, combine the flour, milk, spice, and vanilla in a small bowl, then add to the pot with the bulgur. Simmer until thickened. Add a little water if it becomes too thick.

3 Serve hot with brown sugar and butter, if you like, or anything you'd normally put in oatmeal.

STARKOS

INSPIRED BY **BEYOND GOOD & EVIL**

Beyond Good and Evil is a super fun and underrated game that was published by Ubisoft in 2003. In it, you play Jade, a reporter with some impressive fighting abilities who is charged with uncovering an alien conspiracy. Although the game didn't do well commercially, it has quite a cult following.

Starkos are the primary food source on the planet Hillys and they are found everywhere in the game. When I first saw them, I thought that they looked like a mix between a Jamaican meat patty and an empanada, which makes sense considering aspects of both Jamaican and Latin cultures are in the game—even if they come in the form of rhinoceroses and an A.I. that's just a few missing clothing items away from Agador Spartacus. So, a patty-empanada fusion is exactly what I made and, let me tell you, it's a beautiful thing.

MAKES 20 STARKOS

1 Double-Crust Pie Dough
  (page 8)
1 tablespoon turmeric powder
1 carrot, finely chopped
4 green onions, chopped
1 habanero or Scotch bonnet
  pepper, seeded and chopped
1 cup (150 g) raisins
1 garlic clove, minced
½ cup (67 g) chopped green olives
1 pound (450 g) ground beef
1 tablespoon allspice
½ tablespoon curry powder
½ tablespoon cumin
½ tablespoon dried thyme
Salt and black pepper to taste
2 cups (225 g) shredded Monterey
  Jack cheese

1 Prepare the pie dough, adding the 1 tablespoon turmeric with the dry ingredients in step 1 of that recipe. Chill the dough until needed.

2 In a large skillet over medium heat, stir together the carrot, green onions, pepper, raisins, garlic, olives, and ground beef. Sauté them until they start to brown, about 5 minutes. Add the spices. Stir and spread them around evenly for 10 minutes. Once the veggies are soft and the beef is browned, remove from heat and place the mixture in a mixing bowl. Set aside and let it cool.

3 Preheat oven to 350°F (175°C). Add cheese to the filling mixture and stir to combine.

4 Retrieve the dough from the fridge and cut it into 20 pieces of approximately equal size. Roll each slice out, one piece at a time, into the shape of a square. Add 1–2 tablespoons filling on each square of dough. Fold the dough over the filling to create the triangle shape. Make sure the edges are sealed.

5 Place Starkos onto a baking sheet lined with parchment paper and brush each with butter. Bake them until flaky, approximately 20 minutes.

WHITE DRAGON NOODLES

INSPIRED BY **BLADE RUNNER**

Blade Runner is a 1982 science-fiction film starring Harrison Ford as Rick Deckard, a man whose job as blade runner is to seek out rogue replicants (androids) and eliminate them. The film was based on a novel with my favorite title of all time: *Do Androids Dream of Electric Sheep?* by Phillip K. Dick. It's nice (for me, anyway) when food is central to introducing the protagonist of a story, especially when the scene is so memorable.

When you first see Deckard, he is waiting for a seat at the White Dragon noodle bar, and is shortly called over to take a seat. He orders four of something on the menu, but the chef, speaking Japanese, insists that he only needs two. Deckard gives up on getting four, but adds that he also wants noodles. Visually, the noodles are nondescript, but Deckard seems to thoroughly enjoy them. As soon as he begins to eat, he is arrested. Apparently determined to finish his meal, Deckard continues to eat his noodles in the police car. Eating noodles in the back seat of a flying police car while Edward James Olmos drives may be a dream for some of us, but for Deckard it's an ominous beginning.

SERVES ABOUT 2

8 ounces (225 g) dried soba
  noodles or spaghetti
1½ teaspoon garlic, minced
1 tablespoon mirin
1 tablespoon sake
1 teaspoon dashi powder
3 tablespoons soy sauce
1 teaspoon sesame oil
1 tablespoon rice vinegar
2 tablespoons vegetable oil
White sesame seeds, for topping
Chopped green onions, for topping

1 Cook noodles per package directions. Drain them when they are finished cooking and set aside.

2 In a small bowl, combine all of the ingredients except the noodles, the vegetable oil, and the toppings. Taste and adjust the flavors as necessary.

3 In a large pan or wok, heat the vegetable oil over medium-high heat until it is hot enough to sizzle.

4 Add the cooked noodles, followed shortly by the sauce. Cook for 3–5 minutes, stirring the noodles to make sure they are absorbing the sauce.

5 Serve in a bowl topped with sesame seeds and chopped green onions.

SOUPS AND STEWS

Final Fantasy XIV: **BUTTONS IN A BLANKET**

Mass Effect: **CALAMARI GUMBO**

Minecraft: **MUSHROOM STEW**

The Legend of Zelda: **PUMM'S HOT PUMPKIN SOUP**

Star Wars: **ROOTLEAF SOUP**

Avatar: Legend of Korra: **SEAWEED NOODLES**

Firefly: **WIFE SOUP**

BUTTONS IN A BLANKET

INSPIRED BY FINAL FANTASY XIV

I have been itching to do something from a *Final Fantasy* game. Each game in the series has elements of fantasy and sci-fi and generally revolve around a group of heroes tasked with saving the world. There are many things the series is known for: stunning graphics, epic battles, crazy hairstyles . . . but food? Not so much. Historically, the consumables in the series have, for the most part, been nondescript potions and elixirs. However, the series finally got their chocobos in a row (food wise) and added a lot of tasty-sounding consumables to the MMO and the newest console game.

Buttons in a Blanket is used in the quest "Comfort Me with Mushrooms" and is given as a reward for completing the quests "Just Another Bug Hunt" and "Made to Order." I chose this recipe not only for its adorable name but also because it's very similar to a favorite family recipe of mine. In the game, it's described as "button mushrooms wrapped in parboiled cabbage and stewed in a savory soup." The image in the game shows two stuffed cabbage rolls floating in a red (likely tomato-based) broth.

SERVES 4-6

1 head green cabbage

Filling
½ tablespoon extra-virgin olive oil
1 white onion, chopped
2 cloves garlic, minced
2 cups (200 g) button (white) mushrooms, chopped
1 cup (165 g) wild rice, cooked
1 tablespoon Savory Seasoning Blend (page 12), or to taste
Salt and black pepper, to taste
½ cup (120 ml) white wine

1   Bring a large pot of salted water to a boil. Add the whole cabbage head, reduce the heat to a simmer, and let the cabbage cook for 3–5 minutes until the leaves are soft but not falling apart. Drain and set aside to cool.

2   Prepare the filling. Heat the olive oil in a saucepan over medium heat. Add the onion and sauté until it begins to soften, then add the garlic and sauté for a few more minutes.

3   Add the mushrooms, rice, and seasonings. Cover and cook over medium heat for about 5 minutes. Add the wine and continue to cook until all the liquid has either evaporated or been absorbed.

4   Remove the pan from the heat and set aside to cool to about room temperature or a little higher. Place the cooled filling in a food processor and process until fine. You can also use a knife, but it will take longer. Set aside.

Soup

1 tablespoon olive oil

2 cloves garlic, minced

3 cups (675 g) tomato sauce

2 tablespoons packed brown sugar

2 tablespoons lemon juice

2 tablespoons Worcestershire
  sauce

2 tablespoons Savory Seasoning
  Blend (page 12)

Salt and black pepper, to taste

1½ cups (350 ml) white wine

5   To make the soup, heat the olive oil in a saucepan over medium heat. Add the garlic and cook for 30 seconds. Add all the other ingredients except the wine and stir. Reduce heat to low, then add the wine. Let simmer so the mixture begins to thicken, about 10 minutes.

6   Carefully peel the leaves from the cooled cabbage. You'll only want to use the largest, strongest leaves to make the rolls, the others you can just add to the soup unstuffed, if you like.

7   To assemble the rolls, lay one cabbage leaf out on a flat surface. Place 1–2 tablespoons of filling (how much depends on the size of the leaf) in the center of the leaf. Fold in the sides, and roll up tightly, like a burrito, tucking in the ends. Repeat with the remaining leaves.

8   Pour one-third of the tomato soup in the bottom of a saucepan or Dutch oven. Place each roll seam side down in the soup. Evenly pour the rest of the soup over the tops of the rolls. Cover and let the rolls simmer for 10–20 minutes, or until heated through.

9   To serve, place 2 rolls in a bowl and pour in the soup so it covers the rolls halfway.

CALAMARI GUMBO

INSPIRED BY **MASS EFFECT**

Bioware's *Mass Effect* is one of those games that changes everything. The series follows Commander Shepard and his/her crew as they fight to save the galaxy from the threat of the Reapers, a machine-race bent on destroying the galaxy. To people who haven't played the game, this summarization may seem like your basic sci-fi plot, but *Mass Effect* is anything but basic. It's full of innovative sci-fi goodness, with amazing visuals and superb characters. It's so well developed that it has inspired numerous spin-offs in multiple media, including novels, comics, and film.

There are only two memorable foods in the *Mass Effect* series so far, one of which—Serrice Ice Brandy—I covered in the first cookbook. This one was also mentioned in *Mass Effect 2*, after Shepard retrieves some provisions for the Normandy's cook, Mess Sergeant Gardner. Sgt. Gardner will thank Shepard for providing better food and ask if you want to try his Calamari Gumbo, a recipe he learned from the Asari. Gardner questions why the Asari would have such a recipe, noting it's a bit cannibalistic, but admits the Asari know what they're doing when it comes to cuisine. If you choose to taste the gumbo, you are rewarded with an uncomfortable silence. Yay?

SERVES 8–10

Calamari

1 pound (450 g) squid, cleaned, bodies cut into ¾-inch (2 cm) thick rings, and tentacles left whole
1 tablespoon olive oil
2 tablespoons unsalted butter
2 cloves garlic, minced
1 tablespoon Italian parsley
Salt and black pepper, to taste

1 Pat the squid dry with a paper towel.

2 In a large frying pan, heat the olive oil over high heat until sizzling and just starting to smoke.

3 Carefully add the squid to the pan, making sure the pieces are not touching or piling on top of each other. Add the butter, garlic, and parsley. Season with salt and pepper.

4 Cook, tossing frequently, until the squid is no longer translucent and is cooked all the way through, about a minute or two. Be careful not to overcook the squid. Set it aside.

5 Heat a medium skillet over high heat. Add the andouille sausage and cook until browned on both sides. Set the sausage aside but don't drain the skillet.

Soup

½ pound (225 g) Andouille sausage, sliced into thin discs
1 large yellow onion, finely diced
1 red bell pepper, finely diced
2 ribs celery, finely chopped
2 carrots, peeled and finely diced
5 cloves garlic, minced
½ cup (1 stick, or 120 g) unsalted butter
½ cup (120 g) all-purpose flour
7 cups (1.7 L) fish stock
Salt and black pepper, to taste
Savory Seasoning Blend (page 12), to taste
Cajun seasoning, to taste
½ pound (225 g) okra, sliced into thin discs
Cilantro or Italian parsley, for garnish
Chopped chives, for garnish

6 In the same skillet, cook the onions, bell pepper, celery, carrots, and garlic until soft. Remove from the heat and set aside.

7 Create the roux. In a Dutch oven, melt the butter over medium heat. Gradually sprinkle in the flour, stirring occasionally. Cook the roux until it's a light-caramel color, about 6 or 7 minutes.

8 Add the sautéed vegetables from step 6 to the roux and cook for a few more minutes.

9 In a large saucepan, bring the fish stock to a boil. Once the stock is hot, whisk about 6 cups (1.4 L) of the stock into the roux.

10 In the Dutch oven, bring the soup to a boil, then reduce the heat to a simmer. Add the sausage and okra and continue to simmer for about 20 minutes, adding calamari for the last couple of minutes. You may need to add more stock if the mixture is too thick.

11 Season the soup to taste. Serve and garnish with cilantro, parsley, and green onions.

MUSHROOM STEW

INSPIRED BY **MINECRAFT**

Apparently, you can cook stuff in this game. I wouldn't know. *Minecraft* is a game with seemingly unlimited possibilities, yet somehow I always end up getting killed by nocturnal zombies or shot by skeletons before I can figure out how to build a fire. My lack of *Minecraft* skills isn't important, what is important is that *Minecraft* has inspired a whole genre of mining and crafting games and has hordes of very dedicated fans.

There aren't too many foods in *Minecraft*. I made a recipe for the block cake in the first cookbook, but in this one I wanted to do one of the savory dishes. In the game, you'll get an item called "Mushroom Stew" when you combine the two different kinds of mushrooms with a bowl. You can also obtain the item by milking the mysterious "mooshrooms" creatures that are apparently cow/mushroom hybrids. Oh, to be a fly on the wall during that boardroom meeting. . . . This bowl of fungi restores three of the little drumsticks in your hunger meter. I used beef stock in this to add the "moo" component to stew, but if you don't eat meat please feel free to use mushroom stock.

SERVES 4–6

1 pound (450 g) cremini
   mushrooms
1 pound (450 g) chanterelle or
   oyster mushrooms
2 tablespoons olive oil, divided
Savory Seasoning Blend (page 12),
   to taste
Salt and black pepper, to taste
1 teaspoon chopped fresh thyme
1 teaspoon chopped fresh rosemary
1 teaspoon chopped fresh sage
Pinch red pepper flakes (optional)
4 Roma tomatoes, peeled, seeded,
   and chopped

1 Clean and slice the mushrooms to about ⅛-inch (3 mm) thick slices, but make sure to keep the two mushroom types separate because they will be cooked at different times.

2 Add a tablespoon of olive oil to a skillet and turn the heat to high. Add the creminis and season lightly, then fry for 2–4 minutes or until the mushrooms have a nice brown color.

3 Lower the heat to medium. Add the thyme, rosemary, sage, red pepper flakes, if using, tomatoes, and tomato paste. Stir everything in and cook for 1–2 minutes.

4 Sprinkle with the flour and stir. Cook for 1 more minute, then add the soup base. Taste, and season again, as needed.

5 Add 1 cup (235 ml) of the beef or mushroom broth and stir until thickened, about 1 minute.

1 tablespoon tomato paste
1 tablespoon all-purpose flour
1 Standard Soup Base (page 10)
2 cups (475 ml) beef or mushroom
  broth, divided
1 tablespoon unsalted butter
4 garlic cloves, minced
2 tablespoons parsley, chopped

6 Gradually add the remaining 1 cup (235 ml) broth and cook for another couple minutes. The liquid should have a consistency similar to gravy, so just slowly add the broth as necessary, not all at once. Taste and adjust the seasoning to your preferences.

7 Add the butter and remaining olive oil to a separate skillet over medium-high heat. When the butter begins to brown, add the garlic and chanterelle or oyster mushrooms, season with salt and pepper, and sauté until cooked through and beginning to brown, about 2 minutes.

8 Add the parsley, stir, and cook for another minute.

9 Add the sautéed oyster or chanterelle mushrooms to the cremini mushroom mixture and serve!

67

PUMM'S HOT PUMPKIN SOUP

INSPIRED BY **THE LEGEND OF ZELDA**

I may have gone a tad overboard with the Zelda recipes in the last cookbook. I can't help how I feel, okay? The heart wants what the heart wants. But really, *The Legend of Zelda* is basically the whole reason I started the *Geeky Chef* blog, so it felt right to have a lot of Zelda recipes. Not to mention it's one of the most beloved video game series of all time. I'm practicing more self-control this time around, but I'm still including a recipe in this volume. If you don't like it, play some Zelda and reconsider.

This one appeared in "Skyward Sword." In Pumpkin Landing, one of the sky islands surrounding Skyloft, there is a pub called The Lumpy Pumpkin. There, Link can buy some pumpkin soup from the pub owner, Pumm. Try saying that three times fast. . . . Although this is another pumpkin soup from Zelda (try Yeto's Soup from the blog and the first cookbook), I wanted to make this one its own thing and have a different flavor profile. This recipe is for a warm, comforting, puréed pumpkin soup that's so delicious, you won't even care about all those pots and that really expensive chandelier that Link just broke.

SERVES 2–4

2 sugar pumpkins or 2½ cups (560 g) canned pure pumpkin
2 tablespoons olive oil, plus extra for brushing
5 shallots, peeled and diced
5 cloves garlic, minced
2 cups (475 ml) chicken or vegetable broth
1 cup (235 ml) coconut milk
2 tablespoons pure maple syrup
½ teaspoon allspice
½ teaspoon turmeric
½ teaspoon ground ginger
½ teaspoon thyme

1 Preheat the oven to 350°F (180°C) and line a baking sheet with parchment paper. If using pumpkin purée, proceed straight to step 4.

2 Using a sharp knife, cut off the tops of the sugar pumpkins then halve both the vegetables. Use a sharp spoon to scrape out all of the seeds and strings.

3 Brush the flesh with oil and place the pumpkins face down on the baking sheet. Bake for 45–50 minutes or until a fork easily pierces the skin. Remove from the oven and let cool for 10 minutes, then peel away the skin and set the pumpkins aside.

4 In a large saucepan, add the 2 tablespoons of olive oil, shallots, and garlic. Sauté over medium heat for about 5 minutes, or until slightly browned and translucent.

5 Add all the remaining ingredients and bring to a simmer.

Salt and black pepper, to taste
Savory Seasoning Blend (page 12),
  to taste
Toasted pepitas, to garnish
  (optional)
1 sugar pumpkin, to serve
  (optional)

6 Transfer the soup mixture to a blender and purée the soup,
    then pour the puréed mixture back into the cooking pot.

7 Continue cooking over medium-low heat for about 10 minutes.
    Adjust seasonings to your preference.

8 Serve in a bottle or serve in another sugar pumpkin cut in half
    with the guts removed, if you like.

ROOTLEAF SOUP

INSPIRED BY **STAR WARS**

This little gem flies by so quickly that it's almost unnoticeable. In *Episode V*, Luke meets Yoda for the first time on Dagobah, although Luke doesn't realize that the little green guy is the Jedi Master he is seeking. Honestly, for someone who's apparently very strong in the Force, Luke seems to be a few midi-chlorians short. After some mysterious chitchat, Yoda invites Luke back to his hut, where he is preparing some sort of soup or stew in a cauldron. Yoda calls the soup "rootleaf" as Luke gulps down a bowl of the stuff.

Yoda was stranded on Dagobah after being exiled from the Jedi Order and likely had to make do with very limited resources, so this recipe is appropriately simple. The word "rootleaf" implies something leafy that comes from the ground, so I have chosen some leafy sprouting vegetables and a root vegetable as the stars of this entirely plant-based soup. Enjoy it, you will!

SERVES 6–8

1 Standard Soup Base (page 10)
4 leeks, white and light green parts, thinly sliced
1 head Savoy cabbage, chopped
4 cloves garlic, minced
2 russet potatoes, peeled and chopped
6 cups (1.5 L) vegetable broth
2 fresh bay leaves
3 tablespoons chopped flat-leaf parsley
Savory Seasoning Blend (page 12), to taste
Salt and black pepper, to taste
¼ cup (60 ml) lemon juice

1 Prepare the standard soup base, adding the leeks along with the celery in step 3 of that recipe.

2 Add the cabbage and garlic and cook, stirring occasionally, until the cabbage begins to caramelize, about 10 minutes.

3 Stir in the potatoes, vegetable broth, bay leaves, and parsley. Bring the soup to a simmer and cook, partly covered, until the potatoes begin to fall apart, 45–50 minutes. Add water, if needed, to reach the desired consistency.

4 Season the soup with the savory seasonings, salt and pepper (or anything else you think might taste nice), and stir in the lemon juice just before serving.

SEAWEED NOODLES

INSPIRED BY **AVATAR: LEGEND OF KORRA**

The Last Airbender pushed the envelope of storytelling in family entertainment, but Korra took it even further and went to very unexpected places. *Legend of Korra* takes place in Republic City, seventy years after the events of *The Last Airbender*, in a time when the four elemental societies are united.

In Republic City there's a noodle house in the Little Water Tribe neighborhood. You may remember it as Mako's first date spot of choice and where he goes to eat his feelings later. Their specialty is seaweed noodles, which their advertisements claim are the best in the city. There's no clarification on what exactly seaweed noodles are, but one can surmise that they're noodles made with seaweed, and are most likely served in a savory broth. I tried to use a lot of ingredients that I thought the water tribe would use, but you may have to visit an Asian grocery store to obtain some of them.

SERVES 2–3

Noodles

2 sheets nori
½ cup (120 ml) lukewarm water
4 spinach leaves
2 drops green food dye (optional)
1⅔ cups (170 g) high-gluten flour,
  plus extra for dusting
Pinch salt

Soup

2 cloves garlic, minced
2 teaspoons sesame oil
6 cups (1.4 L) water
3 teaspoons instant dashi
2 pieces kombu
3 dried shiitake mushrooms
½ cup (40 g) dried wakame
1 tablespoon fish sauce, or to taste
1 tablespoon soy sauce, or to taste

1 To prepare the noodles: Tear the nori into small pieces and put in a bowl with the water. Let sit until the nori is basically dissolved into the water. Add this and the spinach leaves into a blender, then blend until uniform. If you want greener noodles, you can blend in the green dye at this point.

2 Add the flour and salt into a large mixing bowl. Pour the seaweed/spinach water slowly, a little at a time, into the bowl with the flour, carefully stirring with a wooden spoon. It should start to form crumbles, which is what you want.

3 Get your hands into the bowl and bring the mixture together into a dough, then knead the dough until it's smooth and elastic, about 10 minutes. At this time, evaluate the dough's color to see if it's green enough for you, keeping in mind the noodles will lose some color when they cook. You can knead in more food dye if you want it a bit greener. If the dough becomes sticky, sprinkle over a little more flour.

4 Cover the dough with a wet cloth and let it rest for about 30 minutes. Transfer the dough to a floured work surface, then roll it into a rectangular shape until it's almost paper-thin.

Suggested Toppings

Green onions
Bonito flakes
Sliced Japanese fish cakes
Furikake

5   Now we're essentially making a jelly roll with the dough. Take one of the edges and fold the dough in by about 2 inches (5 cm). Continue to do this until the dough is completely rolled up, spreading some more flour after each fold to prevent sticking.

6   Cut the folded dough lengthwise into long, thin strips with a sharp knife. Carefully unfold the noodle strips and shake off the extra flour. Lay the noodles out on a baking sheet lined with parchment paper and set aside.

7   Now start to make the stock. In a pot, sauté the minced garlic in the sesame oil for about a minute over medium heat. Add the water, dashi, kombu, and dried mushrooms to the pot and bring to a boil. Once the mushrooms are soft, add the wakame, fish sauce, and soy sauce. You can add more of the sauces if you like things saltier. Remove the kombu, then add the noodles to the soup and let them boil for 2–4 minutes, or until they are tender and cooked through.

8   Serve soup in deep bowls with the toppings of your choice.

WIFE SOUP

INSPIRED BY FIREFLY

This was a show with a great setting, a great cast of characters, and a great story, which was cut down before it even had time to bloom and grow. I'm not crying, you're crying. I know we all probably have some choice Chinese phrases for whoever made the decision to axe this show, but I lamented the loss of *Firefly* plenty in the first cookbook when introducing the recipes for Mudder's Milk and Fruity Oaty Bars, so let's try to focus on the good times, eh browncoats?

"Wife Soup" was made by *Firefly*'s resident badass Zoe, for her whimsical pilot husband, Wash, in the episode *War Stories*. Other than the implication that Wife Soup is very tasty, as Wash only gets treated with it when he's "done good," there aren't any details about what's actually in the soup. However, the color was very green and the texture looked smooth and puréed instead of chunky. So this is silky smooth green vegetable soup—sort of like a cross between split pea and broccoli potato—that can be made vegetarian or not, depending on your whim. This recipe will feed the whole shindig!

SERVES 8–10

1 Standard Soup Base (page 10)
2 cloves garlic, minced
2 russet potatoes, peeled and diced
1 cup (200 g) split peas
4 cups (1 L) chicken or vegetable
  broth
2 cups (350 g) fresh broccoli florets
2 zucchinis, diced
4 cups (200 g) fresh baby spinach
5 fresh basil leaves
1 tablespoon lemon juice
Savory Seasoning Blend (page 12),
  to taste
Pinch cayenne pepper (optional)
Salt and black pepper, to taste

1   In your cooking pot, begin making the soup base, but add the minced garlic when the celery starts to soften in step 3. When the soup base's onions are translucent and the celery softened, add the potatoes, split peas, and broth.

2   Bring the soup to a boil, then reduce the heat to a simmer. Cover the soup and simmer for about 1 hour or until the potatoes and peas are softened.

3   Stir in the broccoli and zucchini. Simmer for 20 more minutes or until the broccoli is tender.

4   Stir in the spinach and basil and remove from the heat.

5   Purée the soup in a blender or food processor. Once thoroughly puréed, stir in the lemon juice and add the Savory Seasoning Blend, cayenne, if using, and salt and pepper to taste.

The Dark Tower: **GUNSLINGER BURRITOS**

Kiki's Delivery Service: **HERRING AND PUMPKIN POT PIE**

Hannibal: **LOIN SERVED WITH A CUMBERLAND SAUCE OF RED FRUITS**

Outlander: **HIGHLAND SANDWICHES**

Breaking Bad: **LOS POLLOS HERMANOS CHICKEN**

American Gods: **MABEL'S PASTIES**

AMBROSIA

INSPIRED BY **THE SIMS**

The Sims is a life-simulation game and is one of the best-selling video games of all time. We all have a different Sims playing style. Some like to have their Sims climb the career ladder without cheating, others just like to build stuff. Personally, I create a Sim version of myself, severely abuse the money cheats, build my dream house, and make a town full of fictional characters to be my friends. Then, I live the dream until I burn out and/or realize my life has fallen apart around me. Totally worth it.

Historically, ambrosia was the food of the gods in Greek mythology. There have been many foods, both real and fictional, that have been given the name ambrosia, including the horrific mushy fruit salad your Aunt Susan brings to Thanksgiving, which makes us all wish there was a ladderless pool we could jump in. Appearing for the first time in *The Sims 3*, Ambrosia is a special food your Sim can make using obscure ingredients. The ingredients were the Death Fish and the Life Fruit. The ingredients in *The Sims 4* were a bit more detailed: Death Flower (made from orchid and pomegranate), Angelfish, and a Potion of Youth. When eaten by a ghost Sim, the deceased Sim will be restored to life.

This recipe is for a pan-fried salmon filet with a pomegranate-hibiscus sauce. Hibiscus represents the flower element and pomegranate is already a great source of antioxidants, thus representing the Potion of Youth. Though fish with flowers and pomegranate might seem like a strange combination, I promise it will be way better than Aunt Susan's ambrosia salad.

SERVES 2

2 center-cut salmon fillets
Salt and black pepper, to taste
2 cups (475 ml) pomegranate juice
2 tablespoons dried hibiscus
2 tablespoons sugar
2 tablespoons apple cider vinegar
1–2 tablespoons cornstarch
Olive oil, for frying
Mint leaves, to garnish (optional)
Julienned beets, to garnish (optional)

1 First cook the fish. Trim off the thinner side of the salmon filets so they have a more square shape. You can reserve the strips for another use, if you like.

2 Season both sides of the fillets with salt, pepper. Set aside.

3 Mix the pomegranate juice, hibiscus, sugar, and vinegar in a medium saucepan. Bring to a boil on medium-high heat and boil for 10 minutes or until the sauce has reduced to about a cup.

4 Strain the dried hibiscus leaves out of the sauce with a strainer or mesh colander, then add the sauce back to the pot.

5   Reduce the heat to medium and slowly sprinkle in 1 tablespoon of the cornstarch and whisk to thicken. If you prefer a thicker sauce, sprinkle in more cornstarch and whisk.

6   Meanwhile, heat the olive oil in a non-stick skillet over medium-high heat.

7   Cook the fish skin-side up in the hot skillet until brown on one side, about 4 minutes. With a spatula, carefully flip the fish over and cook skin-side down until the skin is crisp and the fish is firm and flaky. You may need to do this in batches depending on the size of your skillet.

8   Spoon the sauce onto 2 plates, then add one cooked fillet to each. If desired, garnish the plates with mint leaves and julienned beets.

BEEF AND BACON PIE

INSPIRED BY **ASOIAF/GAME OF THRONES**

For my blog and cookbooks, I try to only take on a very select few dishes from this series. A "best of," if you will. I generally aim for the big obvious ones that are memorable enough to be mentioned in HBO's *Game of Thrones*. For this one, though, there is no special reason for its inclusion other than I just wanted to make it. I mean, it's beef . . . and bacon . . . pie. Not to jump on the old bacon hype train, but pretty much doing that. Beef and bacon pie sounds amazing. Like (SPOILERS!) Joffrey getting poisoned at his own wedding amazing. Maybe even Drogon crashing into Meereen's fighting pits and looking at Daenerys like "get in!" amazing. Sansa's revenge amazing? I could go on . . .

So, the pie only made a couple of very brief appearances in the series. The most memorable of which is when Jon Snow is fleeing the wall to try to join up with Robb Stark after the death of Eddard Stark. Feeling particularly homesick, he wishes he could hear Bran's laugh or one of Old Nan's stories, or eat one of Gage's (the head cook of Winterfell) Beef and Bacon pies. So, let's try Jon Snow's comfort food of choice.

SERVES 6-8

1 pound (450 g) stew beef, cubed
Salt and black pepper, to taste
2 tablespoons olive oil
10 strips thick-cut bacon, diced
2 carrots, roughly chopped
1 yellow onion, chopped
1 cup (235 ml) red wine
1 cup (235 ml) beef broth
1 cup (150 g) raisins
2 bay leaves
1 teaspoon chopped fresh thyme
½ teaspoon ground allspice
1 Double-Crust Pie Dough (page 8)
1 tablespoon flour, for dusting

1   Preheat oven to 325°F (170°C) and season the beef with salt and pepper.

2   In a Dutch oven, brown the beef in the olive oil until it's got some good color on all sides. Remove and set aside.

3   Add the bacon to the Dutch oven and cook until crispy. Remove with a slotted spoon and set the bacon aside, leaving the fat behind.

4   Add the carrots to the bacon fat and sauté until they are softened, then add the onion. Keep cooking until the onion is soft and beginning to caramelize.

5   Add back the beef, along with the red wine, beef broth, raisins, herbs, and spices. Use a wooden spoon to scrape up any brown bits sticking to the pot and incorporate them with the broth and wine.

6   Cover the Dutch oven with the lid and stick it in the oven to braise for 1–2 hours or until the beef is tender enough that it can be mashed with a fork.

7   Break the beef up into smaller pieces—this will help incorporate the gravy. Once done, stir in the bacon.

8   Increase the oven temperature to 375°F (190°C) and roll out the pie dough on a lightly floured surface. Grease and line two 12 ounce ramekins with pie dough, keeping in mind that there should be enough dough left over to top them as well. Trim away the excess.

9   Spoon the beef mixture into each dough-lined ramekin, rationing it evenly between the pies.

10 Roll out the dough again and top each of the ramekins with a layer of dough, cutting off any excess and rerolling as necessary. Crimp the edges of the pie to seal and cut vents into the center.

11 Bake the pies for about 25 minutes, or until the crust is a nice golden brown color.

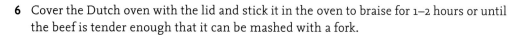

DOUBLEMEAT MEDLEY

INSPIRED BY BUFFY THE VAMPIRE SLAYER

Buffy the Vampire Slayer is absolutely beloved by its fans. We all wished we could be part of the Scooby Gang: reading big tomes, casting spells, staking vamps, and just generally saving the world a lot. Expanding on the horror-comedy film of the same name, the *BtVS* series took the story of the vampire slayer (a young girl chosen to fight the forces of evil) to a whole new level. The show was a game-changer for fantasy horror–based television, slaying all expectations while effortlessly walking the tightrope of being terrifying, poignant, and wickedly funny—sometimes all at once.

In the most painful season, the Slayer is forced to face a new beast: the minimum-wage fast-food job. It doesn't take long for Buffy to sense that there's something weird going on at the Doublemeat Palace. Employees periodically disappear and there's a mysterious ingredient described only as a "meat process." Naturally, Buffy assumes her coworkers are becoming the secret ingredient. However, the truth is, while her coworkers are being eaten by a demon, the "meat" at the Doublemeat Palace is actually just processed vegetables. I give you, The Doublemeat Medley: a classic double-decker with a twist. A veggie-beef patty above the mid-bun and a slice of veggie-chicken product below the mid-bun. Plus pickles!

MAKES 2 MEDLEYS

Chicken Patty

8 ounces (225 g) extra-firm tofu,
  drained and crumbled
½ tablespoon white miso
½ tablespoon soy sauce
½ teaspoon chicken-style
  seasoning
Savory Seasoning Blend (page 12),
  to taste
Salt and black pepper, to taste

Beef Patty

8 ounces (225 g) veggie ground beef
½ tablespoon nutritional yeast

1 First make the "chicken" patty. Combine all the ingredients in a food processor or in a bowl using an immersion blender.

2 Line a colander with cheesecloth. Scoop the tofu mixture into the cheesecloth and wrap it up. Place a plate on the bundle and add a heavy object (like a big can of something) on top.

3 Put the colander into a large bowl and refrigerate for at least 4 hours, but overnight is best. This allows the tofu to drain and the flavors to permeate.

4 Preheat the oven to 375°F (190°C). Line a baking sheet with parchment paper. Scoop out the tofu mixture and form into 2 disks or patties. Bake on the lined baking sheet for 20 minutes, or until lightly browned.

3 tablespoons breadcrumbs
Dash Worcestershire sauce
3 tablespoons onion, minced
Savory Seasoning Blend (page 12), to taste
Salt and black pepper, to taste
1 tablespoon cornstarch

Burger Assembly
Ketchup
Mustard
Mayo
4 sesame seed buns
Pickles, sandwich sliced
White onion, thinly sliced
Green leaf lettuce leaves
Sliced cheese
Hothouse tomato, sliced

5 Meanwhile, make the "beef" patty. Mix all the ingredients together in a mixing bowl, then form into 2 patties.

6 Heat some oil in a frying pan over medium-high heat. Fry the "beef" patties for 3 minutes on each side, or until they have a nice color on the outside.

7 Now assemble the burger. Spread the condiments on the bottom part of the bun. In this order, top the bun base with pickles, then some onions, a lettuce leaf, then the chicken patty, then the cheese. Top with more condiments.

8 On top of the chicken patty with condiments, place another bottom bun. On this bun spread some condiments, a lettuce leaf, the tomato, then the beef patty. Top the beef patty with condiments and finish with the top bun. Repeat the process for the other burger.

GUNSLINGER BURRITOS

INSPIRED BY **THE DARK TOWER**

The Dark Tower was Stephen King's epic fantasy. It follows Roland, a gunslinger, and his four companions as they quest to find the Dark Tower. The Dark Tower is basically the center-point of all dimensions, the glue that holds many universes together. During the ka-tets adventures, Roland takes whatever meat and non-poisonous plants they can find and wraps them in edible leaves. Eddie refers to these as "Gunslinger Burritos." These aren't supposed to be very tasty (they're more for necessity than enjoyment), but we'll try out one of these burritos on what might have been a particularly good day.

In "The Drawing of the Three," Roland shoots a deer, which provided the ka-tet with some much-needed meat. Roland also had a salt lick, which he kept around for curing meat. Wild onions, garlic, and mushrooms are relatively easy to find and harvest when on a journey. Feel free to make any substitutions or additions you like, as Roland would use whatever the ka-tet had available at the time. Do not slice with your hands—he who slices with his hands has forgotten the face of his father . . .

SERVES 2

8 ounces (225 g) venison backstrap or other lean game meat, trimmed and brought to room temperature
19 pinches (1 teaspoon) salt
1 tablespoon lard or other animal fat
¼ cup (40 g) wild onion or 2 green onions, chopped
1 teaspoon wild garlic or 1 clove regular garlic, minced
1 cup (100 g) porcini or chanterelle mushrooms, sliced
2 large collard green leaves, stems removed

1 Brine the venison by coating it with the salt and set aside at room temperature for 1 hour. Then shake off the salt and pat the steaks dry with a paper towel.

2 Preheat the grill or a griddle to hot, then grill the steaks for 15–20 minutes or until medium to medium-rare. Test the steak using your fingers—if it's too soft when you poke it, it's not done, and if it's hard when you poke it, it's overdone. You want just a bit of give when you poke it. When done, let the steak rest.

3 Melt the lard or other fat in a skillet on medium-high heat, then add the onions and garlic and sauté until they soften. Add the mushrooms and cook until they are brown and juicy.

4 Now that the steak has rested, slice it into ½-inch (13 mm) slices.

5 Now construct the Gunslinger Burrito. Take each collard green leaf and spread it out. Top with the sliced venison and the sautéed onions, garlic, and mushrooms. Roll up like a burrito and eat like a gunslinger!

HERRING AND PUMPKIN POT PIE

INSPIRED BY KIKI'S DELIVERY SERVICE

Kiki's Delivery Service is the Studio Ghibli film based on the book *Majo no Takkyūbin* by Eiko Kadono, which was adapted and directed by Hayao Miyazaki in 1989. Studio Ghibli is now famous worldwide for its beautiful animations but at the time it gained some attention for its delicious depictions of food, which are absolutely mouth-watering. Let's be real, if I was in *Spirited Away*, I probably would have gone on a gluttony-fueled rampage like No-Face and/or suffered the same fate as Chihiro's parents and regretted nothing.

Kiki's Delivery Service has less food moments than some other Ghibli films, but it does have an awesome talking cat and this very memorable pie. In the film, Kiki is a witch, and witches eventually leave their hometown to find their very own town to serve and protect, using their unique witchy abilities. Kiki's only known ability is flying, so when she finds her town, she finds herself offering a delivery service. One of her customers is a sweet old lady who needs Kiki's help delivering a herring and pumpkin pot pie to her granddaughter's birthday party. Herring is definitely an acquired taste, but the pie looks warm and comforting, is dotted with black olives, and has a little fish design in the dough.

SERVES 6–8

2 tablespoons unsalted butter
2 tablespoons all-purpose flour,
  plus extra for dusting
1¼ cups (300 ml) whole milk,
  heated to 100–110°F (38–43°C)
Salt and black pepper, to taste
Olive or vegetable oil, for frying
1 white onion, chopped
1 kabocha pumpkin, steamed and
  peeled

1   Melt the butter in a heavy-bottomed saucepan. Stir in the flour and cook over medium heat, stirring constantly, until it bubbles, but don't let it get brown, around 2 minutes.

2   Add the milk, stirring as the sauce thickens. Bring to a boil, add salt and pepper to taste, lower the heat and cook, stirring, for 2–3 minutes more. Remove from the heat. Set aside.

3   Put some oil in a frying pan and sauté the onion until aromatic and translucent. Cut the pumpkin into largish chunks, add salt and pepper, then briefly sauté those as well with the onion so they absorb some flavor.

continued ▶▶

3 ounces (75 g) smoked herring
fillets*, drained and fillets chopped
very small
2 Double-Crust Pie Dough
(page 8)
2 cups (230 g) sharp white
Cheddar cheese, shredded
10 black olives

* Let's face it, many people find the taste
and texture of herring gross. That's
okay; it's an acquired taste. If you can't
stomach the thought of herring, hot
smoked salmon will do nicely instead.

4   Add the chopped fillets and the sauce to the pumpkin and
onion and stir everything together. You don't want to mix, just
stir enough to coat everything in the sauce. Season again with
salt and pepper, or any other seasoning that takes your fancy.

5   On a floured surface, roll out about half the dough so it's
big enough to cover a standard rectangular casserole dish.
Grease the casserole dish and line it with the rolled-out
dough. Cut off the excess and set aside.

6   Pour or spoon the pumpkin/herring mixture into the pastry
lined casserole dish. Use a spoon to spread it out so it covers
the surface evenly. Sprinkle the white Cheddar on top of the
mixture, so it covers it as much as possible.

7   Roll out the remaining dough and cover the top. Puncture
the dough all over with something sharp and pointy to create
vents. You should have a good amount of dough left over,
which will be used to make the design. This is a good time to
turn on your oven to preheat to 375°F (190°C).

8   For the decorating, I highly recommend looking at a picture
of the pie online, or pausing your copy of the film. Take the
leftover dough and roll it again. Cut 5–6 strips from it, about
an inch or so wide. Place them on top of the pie, diagonally,
one at a time with some space between, to create the water
design. Cut off the excess. On the end of each strip, place a
black olive and push it into the dough a bit.

9   Cut a fish shape from the rolled-out dough. Place that in the
center of the pie on top of the lines. Using whatever dough is
left over, add the fins, eyes, mouth, and "scales." Use a knife
to create the indents on the tail and fins.

10 Bake the pie for about 25 minutes, or until the top crust is
golden brown but not burnt. Use your oven light to check on
the pie periodically to make sure it's not burning. You did it!

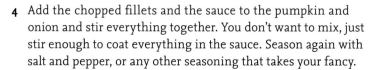

LOIN SERVED WITH A CUMBERLAND SAUCE OF RED FRUITS

INSPIRED BY **HANNIBAL**

The *Hannibal* series is a rare instance of an adaption that actually adds to its source material. I've been a huge fan of the Thomas Harris books and the films for quite some time, but the TV show took the series to new, even more disturbing places. Not only that, it's taken Hannibal's food game well beyond fava beans and Chianti (or Amarone, for book fans).

There are three important things to remember about Hannibal Lecter: he hates rude people; he can manipulate a person to eat their own face; he has very expensive taste. He often uses ingredients that are, shall we say, difficult to obtain? In the TV series, Hannibal has served his friends and acquaintances everything from black chicken soup to blood puddings, and, of course, their own appendages. I chose this dish, from the Season 1 episode "Amuse-Bouche," for its relative simplicity. Hannibal tells Crawford that the "loin" is served in "a Cumberland sauce of red fruits." Of course, the "loin" is really, definitely, going to be pork this time.

SERVES 4–6

Pork Loin

¼ cup (60 ml) extra-virgin olive oil
¼ cup (60 ml) soy sauce
2 cloves garlic, minced
3 tablespoons Dijon honey mustard
Savory Seasoning Blend (page 12), to taste
Salt and black pepper, to taste
1–2 pounds (450–900 g) boneless pork loin roast, on the thicker side

1 For the pork, whisk together the olive oil, soy sauce, garlic, mustard, Seasoning Blend, salt, and pepper in a bowl. Place the pork loin in a large resealable plastic bag and pour in the marinade. Marinate in the refrigerator at least 1 hour.

2 While the pork marinates, prepare the sauce. Zest the orange and the lemon. Place the fruit rinds in a medium saucepan and cover with some water. Bring to a boil over medium-high heat, then reduce the heat to medium and simmer, stirring occasionally, for 5 minutes, or until the rinds soften. Drain the liquid, but keep the rinds.

continued >>

Sauce

1 orange
1 lemon
⅔ cup (200 g) red currant jelly*
½ cup (120 ml) port wine
1 tablespoon red wine vinegar
½ teaspoon mustard powder
½ teaspoon ground ginger
½ teaspoon cornstarch
Salt and black pepper, to taste

* Really, *really* not trying to be rude to Hannibal Lecter here, but saying "a Cumberland sauce of red fruits" is kind of redundant, since Cumberland sauce is usually made with red currants. Hopefully he won't reward this small criticism by having me at one of his lavish dinner parties. Cranberry sauce or lingonberry jelly will work if you can't find red currant jelly.

Side

1 shallot, minced
2 teaspoons Dijon mustard
2 tablespoons white wine vinegar
½ cup (120 ml) extra-virgin olive oil
Salt and black pepper, to taste
1 pound (350 g) haricot vert or
   green beans, lightly steamed
½ cup (25 g) Bleu d'Auvergne or
   other blue cheese, crumbled
¼ cup (30 g) walnuts, toasted

3 Squeeze the juice from the orange and lemon and add to the rinds with the jelly, wine, vinegar, mustard powder, and ginger. Cook, stirring, over medium heat for 3–5 minutes. Reduce heat to low and simmer, stirring occasionally, for 6–8 minutes, or until the sauce thickens slightly.

4 Combine the cornstarch and a couple tablespoons of water. Add the cornstarch mixture to the sauce and cook, stirring constantly, over medium heat, for about a minute, or until the mixture thickens slightly. Season with salt and pepper. Transfer to a heatproof serving jug and let cool to about room temperature.

5 Preheat the oven to 350°F (180°C). Transfer the pork loin to a baking dish; pour the marinade over the pork. Cook in the oven until the pork is no longer pink in the center, 45–60 minutes. A meat thermometer inserted into the center should read 145°F (62°C). Let the pork rest while you move on to the side.

6 Whisk together the shallot, mustard, vinegar, olive oil, and salt and pepper. Toss the steamed green beans with the dressing. Top with blue cheese and chopped walnuts. Season with salt and pepper if necessary.

7 Add the green beans to your serving plates. Slice the loin very thin, about ½-inch (1 cm) thick, and add to the serving plate. Pour the sauce over the loin and enjoy!

HIGHLAND SANDWICHES

INSPIRED BY **OUTLANDER**

To some minds, the whole icky romance thing takes *Outlander* firmly out of geek territory. However, if we can collectively pretend that the bodice-ripping element doesn't exist, *Outlander* is essentially a fantasy story about time travel, which is unambiguously geeky. Not only that, but the screen adaption is headed by none other than Ronald D. Moore, of *Star Trek* and *Battlestar Galactica* fame.

Much of the *Outlander* series takes place in the Scottish Highlands, so the culture of eighteenth-century Scotland is a huge part of the story's setting, including the cuisine. Bannocks, brose, and haggis are just some of the traditional foods that make an appearance. One tasty-sounding treat, which has roots in Scottish tradition but is mostly unique to the *Outlander* series, is what the protagonist, Claire, calls a Highland Sandwich. Appearing in the third book, it is described as a loaf of freshly baked bread stuffed with sheep's cheese and homemade pickle. For the fresh bread, I opted for Scottish baps, or morning rolls, which lend themselves perfectly to sandwiches, with Scottish chutney and fresh sheep cheese.

SERVES 4

Pickle/Chutney

2 medium yellow onions, peeled and finely chopped

2 McIntosh apples, peeled, cored, and roughly chopped

¼ cup (37 g) raisins, sultanas, and/or currants

2 teaspoons peeled and grated fresh ginger

¾ cup (170 g) packed light brown sugar

½ cup (120 ml) malt vinegar

½ cup (120 ml) apple cider vinegar

3 teaspoons Sweet Spice Blend (page 12), or to taste

Salt and black pepper, to taste

1 sterilized canning jar

1 First, you'll need to prepare the pickle/chutney, which will need at least a week or two to mature. Place all the pickle ingredients (except the jar!) into a large pan. Bring slowly to a boil and then lower the heat to a rolling boil. Stir the chutney regularly and make sure it does not burn.

2 Cook until it is the consistency of a thick jam and all the liquids have dissolved. Spoon the hot pickle into a hot and sterile jar (you can either boil the jar or use the sterilize feature on a dishwasher) and seal immediately. Store in a cool and dark place and leave to mature for at least a week.

3 Now it's time to make the bread. Preheat the oven to 400°F (200°C). Rub the butter into the flour, then make a well in the center. In a small mixing bowl, mix the yeast with the sugar, then add the milk and salt, and let sit for a few minutes. Then pour the yeast mixture into the well.

Baps

2 tablespoons butter

1¾ cups (220 g) bread flour, plus extra for dusting

2½ teaspoons fresh yeast

1 teaspoon granulated sugar

½ cup (120 ml) milk, room temperature, plus extra for brushing

½ teaspoon salt

Fresh sheep's milk cheese*, to taste

* Fresh sheep's milk cheese is seasonal and difficult to find. There are several online retailers that sell it, or try grocery stores that sell local or specialty cheeses. If you absolutely cannot find it, thoroughly mix ricotta with chèvre, at a 2:1 ratio, and you'll have an acceptable approximation.

4   Mix to a dough, adding extra warm milk if required. Cover the dough with plastic wrap or a light cloth and allow to rise until doubled in bulk, for about an hour or two depending on the temperature of your kitchen.

5   Knead the dough, and divide evenly into four pieces. Knead each into a ball about the size of a fist, and flatten with your hand, then lightly roll to a round with a rolling pin. Place the dough balls on a well-floured baking tray. Brush with milk and sprinkle flour all over the tops. Allow to rise for another 20 minutes.

6   Bake in the oven for 10 minutes, or until golden brown and firm to the touch. Dust with more flour and allow them to cool a bit on a wire rack.

7   Time to assemble the sandwich! Cut a bap in half horizontally from the middle. Spread the sheep's cheese over the bottom half and top with the relish. Finish the sandwich with the top half of the bap. Repeat for each bap. Enjoy!

LOS POLLOS HERMANOS CHICKEN

INSPIRED BY **BREAKING BAD**

Yo, yo, yo! 1-4-8-3 to the 3 to the 6 to the 9. Representin' the ABQ! This offering is from everyone's favorite fictional fast-food joint that's actually a cover for a giant meth operation, Los Pollos Hermanos. Unlike most drug fronts, Los Pollos Hermanos, a chain of fast-food restaurants specializing in fried chicken, are actually quality establishments. This is because Gustavo Fring, the owner, is as meticulous in the running of his restaurant operation as he is in the running of his meth operation. It's almost as if there aren't large amounts of meth hidden in the barrels of fry batter.

The chicken at Los Pollos Hermanos has a Latin flare, so this is some flavorful and spicy fried chicken. As always with deep frying, you'll probably end up in a sticky situation, and may need to call for help (dial 505-503-4455!). While you will certainly get dirty, the means justify the ends. With a spicy, crispy exterior and a tender interior, I think you'll find that this chicken tastes much better than roof pizza.

SERVES 2

½ cup (120 ml) lime juice
½ cup (120 ml) orange juice
8 ounces (225 g) sour cream
2 cloves garlic, minced
1 teaspoon chili powder, divided
1 teaspoon ground cumin, divided
Cayenne pepper, to taste
Savory Seasoning Blend (page 12), to taste
1 teaspoon dried oregano
Salt and black pepper, to taste
4 chicken tenders
2 eggs, large

1 Combine the lime juice, orange juice, sour cream, minced garlic, half a teaspoon of each spice, the oregano, and some salt and pepper in a non-reactive bowl, then add the chicken tenders and toss to coat. Let the chicken marinate in the fridge, covered, for at least 2 hours, but overnight is best. When ready to cook, let the chicken sit at room temperature for about 20 minutes before breading.

2 In a bowl, whisk together the eggs and the hot sauce, if using, until the mixture turns bright orange. In a separate bowl, sift together both flours, the remaining spices and seasonings, and some salt and pepper.

3 Set up your deep fryer with your frying oil of choice, then heat the oil to 350°F (190°C). You may also use a cast-iron skillet or other high-temperature pot for frying.

Hot sauce, to taste (optional)
1 cup (125 g) all-purpose flour
1 cup (120 g) corn flour
High-smoke-point oil or lard,
**   for deep frying**

4 Dip the marinated chicken in the egg mixture, and then coat well in the flour mixture.

5 Fry the chicken in the oil until brown and crisp, 8–10 minutes. You may need to do this in batches depending on the size of your deep fryer or pot. Use tongs to turn the chicken to make sure it is getting fried evenly, gently rotating it occasionally.

6 Place the fried chicken on a wire rack or paper towel to rest for about 10 minutes before serving.

MABEL'S PASTIES

INSPIRED BY AMERICAN GODS

Neil Gaiman's *American Gods* is one of my all-time favorite books. Full disclosure: I spent much of my teen years holed up in my room reading and rereading Neil Gaiman books and comics. Out of all of Neil Gaiman's fantastic novels, *American Gods* spoke to me the most. It follows Shadow Moon, an ex-convict who, after being released from prison, finds himself plunged into the middle of a very strange war between the gods of our ancestors and new gods we've created for ourselves in America.

Somewhere in the middle of the book, Shadow spends a few months lying low in the fictional, almost-too-nice town of Lakeside, Wisconsin. In Lakeside, the local eatery is run by the very gregarious Mabel, who is "famous" for her pasties. As mentioned in the novel, pasties made their way to Michigan's Upper Peninsula area in the 1800s along with the influx of Cornish miners, and now the area sees more than a few bastardized versions of the traditional hand pie. Shadow describes Mabel's pasties as "a savory delight wrapped in hot pastry" and notes that they contain meat, potatoes, carrots, and onions. I don't know about you, but chances are that if you stick that in pie crust, I will like it. Enjoy these bad boys at breakfast with some hot chocolate and the local morning paper, which may or may not have a missing children's section.

MAKES 4 PASTIES

1 large russet potato, peeled and
  chopped small
2 carrots, peeled and finely chopped
½ yellow onion, chopped
1 pound (450 g) lean ground beef
Savory Seasoning Blend (page 12),
  to taste
2 Double-Crust Pie Dough (page 8)
Salt and black pepper, to taste

1 Preheat oven to 350°F (180°C).

2 In a large mixing bowl, add all the ingredients except the pie dough and stir together.

3 Separate the dough into four equal pieces and roll it out into 6-inch (15 cm) circles.

4 Add the filling to the center of each pie disk.

5 Fold the disk over to create a semi-circular pocket. Wet your fingers and crimp the edges together to seal.

6 Cut small slits into the center of the dough to vent.

7 Place the pies on a parchment-lined baking sheet and bake for 35–40 minutes, or until the dough is golden brown.

CAKES AND CUPCAKES

Doctor Who: **BALL BEARING CAKES**

The Elder Scrolls Online: **CREAM CHEESE FROSTED GORAPPLE CAKE**

Divergent: **DAUNTLESS CHOCOLATE CAKE**

The Wheel of Time: **HONEYCAKES**

His Dark Materials: **MARCHPANE CAKE**

Harry Potter: **ROCK CAKES**

The Hobbit: **SEED CAKES**

BALL BEARING CAKES

INSPIRED BY DOCTOR WHO

Oddly, edible ball bearings are some sort of long-running joke in *Doctor Who*, starting all the way back with the Fourth Doctor. In the fifteenth season of the classic series, the Fourth Doctor was eating a bag of sweets (most likely Jelly Babies, as per usual) and jokingly asked K9 if he'd like a ball bearing. Later, the Fourth Doctor seemed to have developed a liking for edible ball bearings himself. The Doctor's tenth incarnation also loved edible ball bearings, calling them "genius" and stating "No other species in the galaxy has ever bothered to make them." That's us, making our food look like things that aren't food. Why are we like this?

The Tenth Doctor mentioned getting little cakes with crunchy ball bearings on top at tea parties in the '40s. One of my favorite things to make is floral- or herbal-flavored cakes and frostings, and I have found that bergamot and rose go really well together. As the Doctor said, he remembers these being served at a tea party, and his companion at the time was Rose, so it seemed the perfect time to break out this lovely flavor combo.

MAKES 12 CUPCAKES

Cake
1 Yellow Cake Mix (page 9)
1 tablespoon Earl Grey tea leaves, finely ground

Rose Frosting
½ cup (1 stick, or 120 g) unsalted butter, softened
3 cups (375 g) confectioner's sugar, divided
1 tablespoon rose water

Topping
Silver dragee balls (a.k.a. Edible Ball Bearings)

1 Prepare the Yellow Cake Mix, adding the ground tea leaves to the recipe along with the flour, baking powder, and salt in step 4 of that recipe. In step 9, transfer the batter into 2 muffin/cupcake tins. When the cakes are almost cool, begin preparing the frosting.

2 Begin making the frosting by beating the butter and 2 cups (250 g) of the sugar together until thick.

3 Add the rose water to the frosting along with the remaining cup (125 g) of sugar.

4 Continue to beat until the frosting becomes light and fluffy.

5 Spread the frosting onto the cooled cakes ASAP before the frosting hardens and top with edible ball bearings.

CREAM CHEESE FROSTED GORAPPLE CAKE

INSPIRED BY **THE ELDER SCROLLS ONLINE**

After dedicating years to *World of Warcraft*, *Guild Wars 2*, and even this really obscure Korean MMO called *ROSE Online*, I told myself I would never, ever play another MMO. . . . But then Bethesda went and had an *ESO* sale. And I'm a sucker for an *Elder Scrolls* game. Unfortunately for my productivity, *ESO* is just like any other Elder Scrolls game, with gorgeous scenery, interesting lore, fun gameplay, and a lot of detail. Yep, just like every other Elder Scrolls game . . . except there's no real ending and you can just keep playing it indefinitely. Bye, bye social life! See ya later, hopes and dreams!

There are lots of intriguing foods in *ESO*. I chose this recipe because I owe it a debt for getting me from level 35 to level 40 with minimal death and wasted soul gems. And it just sounds really tasty. Honestly, though, the Elder Scrolls series has been coming through with tasty-sounding foods for years. I could easily write an entire Elder Scrolls cookbook.* The in-game recipe just includes carrot, apple, and flour, so we're going to embellish it a bit to make this work.

* Bethesda, hit me up.

SERVES 8–10

Cake

¾ cup (1½ sticks, or 180 g) unsalted butter, softened
¾ cup (150 g) granulated sugar
¼ cup (60 g) packed light brown sugar
2 large eggs
1 cup (125 g) all-purpose flour
Sweet Spice Blend (page 12), to taste
½ teaspoon baking powder
¼ teaspoon baking soda

1 Preheat the oven to 350°F (180°C) and grease a 9-inch (23 cm) baking pan.

2 In a mixing bowl, cream together the butter and sugars. Add the eggs and beat for another minute until incorporated and fluffy.

3 Combine the flour, spices, baking powder, baking soda, and salt; gradually add to the egg/butter/sugar mixture just until combined. Stir in the shredded carrot and apple.

4 Spoon the batter into the greased baking pan and bake for 25–30 minutes, or until a toothpick inserted near the center of the cake comes out clean. Let the cake cool and set before removing it from the pan for frosting.

Pinch salt

2 carrots, peeled and finely
shredded

2 apples (any kind) peeled, cored,
and shredded

Frosting

3 ounces (85 g) cream cheese,
softened

1¼ cups (155 g) confectioner's sugar

1 tablespoon unsalted butter, softened

1 teaspoon lemon juice

¼ teaspoon vanilla extract

Red and orange gel food dye

5   After the cake is almost completely cool, prepare the frosting.
In a clean mixing bowl, combine all the frosting ingredients
and beat until smooth. You may need to keep adding the food
coloring at a 2:1 red to orange ratio until the frosting has that
burnt orange color it has in the game. Spread over the cake
with an icing spatula or frosting tool.

DAUNTLESS CHOCOLATE CAKE

INSPIRED BY **DIVERGENT**

The *Divergent* series is a trilogy of YA dystopian novels, written by Veronica Roth, set in post-apocalyptic Chicago, in a time when society is split into five factions, which each exemplify a set of personality traits. The story follows Beatrice "Tris" Prior as she comes of age and must decide which faction she belongs in. She chooses the Dauntless faction, who value fearlessness and cool tattoos. Although later she discovers she is Divergent, which means she possesses qualities from more than one faction . . . but that's beside the point, and the point is cake.

The Dauntless faction is known for things like wearing black leather, jumping off buildings, and their delicious chocolate cake. This cake is referenced frequently in the series, and always positively. But be warned, this dessert isn't for pansycakes; it's rich, decadent, and with the secret ingredient, hot coffee, it'll get you juiced up for some extreme parkour.

SERVES 8–10

Cake

1¾ cups (215 g) all-purpose flour, plus extra for dusting
2 cups (400 g) granulated sugar
¾ cup (78 g) unsweetened cocoa powder
1½ teaspoons baking powder
1½ teaspoons baking soda
Pinch salt
2 eggs
1 cup (235 ml) whole milk
½ cup (120 ml) vegetable oil
2 teaspoons vanilla extract
1 cup (235 ml) hot coffee

1 Preheat oven to 350°F (180°C). Grease and sprinkle flour onto the bottom of two 9-inch (23 cm) cake pans.

2 In a medium-sized mixing bowl, stir together the flour, sugar, cocoa powder, baking powder, baking soda, and salt.

3 In a separate bowl, mix the eggs, milk, oil, and vanilla with a hand mixer.

4 Add the wet ingredients to the dry ingredients and mix for 3 minutes with the mixer. Stir in the hot coffee with a wooden spoon.

5 Pour the batter evenly into the two cake pans. Bake for 30–35 minutes, or until a toothpick inserted in the center comes out clean. Cool for 20 minutes before removing from pans to cool completely.

Frosting

½ cup (1 stick, or 120 g) unsalted butter, softened

1½ cups (165 g) unsweetened cocoa powder

⅓ cup (80 ml) whole milk, plus a little extra

1 teaspoon vanilla extract

2½ cups (310 g) confectioner's sugar

Topping

Your favorite decorations

6   Just before the cakes are completely cool, begin the frosting. In a large bowl, beat the butter and cocoa powder together. Add the ⅓ cup milk and vanilla and beat until smooth. Gradually beat in the confectioner's sugar until the desired consistency is achieved.

7   Line your cake board or serving piece with parchment paper and carefully place one of the cakes down onto it. If your cake has a rounded top, trim this off with a sharp knife so it's flat and place this side down. Using a frosting spatula or a knife, spread the frosting evenly on top of the bottom cake layer.

8   Take the other cake (again, if it's rounded on top, trim off the rounded part) and gently place it, trimmed side down, on the frosted layer.

9   Take about a ½ cup (100 g) of frosting and thin it out with a little milk so it spreads a little easier. Spread a thin frosting layer on the tops and sides of the cake, then chill until set, about 15 minutes. If you can still see any cake, repeat this step.

10 Now, frost the cake with the regular, unthinned frosting. Start with the top of the cake, spreading the frosting all the way to the edge of the layer. Then, frost the sides. If you have a turntable, you can spin it around as you frost for a more even coating. When you're done, remove the parchment paper. Place any decorations on the cake that you wish.

HONEYCAKES

INSPIRED BY **THE WHEEL OF TIME**

The Wheel of Time series, initially written by the late Robert Jordan and completed by Brandon Sanderson, is one of the greatest epic fantasies of all time. But the real question is, how's the food?

Honeycakes are one of the first foods mentioned in *The Eye of the World*, the first book of the series. Before fate fell upon Rand and his companions, they were mostly concerned with sheepherder things—like girls and Mistress al'Vere's honeycakes. Although not as important as stopping Shai'tan's evil plans, these cakes definitely deserve some attention. These treats are heavenly—the honey syrup soaks into the cake and oozes with every bite, and they pair well with spiced wine and fresh fruits . . . but perhaps avoid peaches?

SERVES 10–12

Cake

2 large eggs
⅔ cup (230 g) orange blossom honey
1 teaspoon vanilla extract
1½ cups (185 g) all-purpose flour
Sweet Spice Blend (page 12), to taste
1 tablespoon orange zest
2 teaspoons baking powder
Pinch baking soda
1 teaspoon salt
1 cup (120 g) heavy whipping cream

Honey Syrup

1 cup (350 g) honey
½ cup (100 g) granulated sugar
¾ cup (180 ml) water
1 teaspoon lemon juice

1 Preheat oven to 325°F (170°C) and grease 6 ramekins or individual cake pans, or a standard-size muffin tin.

2 Beat the eggs in a mixing bowl until foamy and thick, then add the honey and vanilla. Mix well.

3 In a separate bowl, sift together the flour, Sweet Spice Blend, zest, baking powder, baking soda, and salt.

4 Add one-third of the dry mixture, then one-third of the cream to the egg mixture. Mix well and repeat until everything is combined. Pour the batter evenly into ramekins, cake pans, or a standard-size muffin tin. Bake for 20–30 minutes, or until a toothpick inserted in the center comes out clean. Let cool.

5 While the cakes cool, work on the honey syrup. In a saucepan, combine the honey, sugar, and water. Bring to a simmer for around 5 minutes. Stir in the lemon juice, bring to a boil and boil for another couple of minutes.

6 Poke the cakes multiple times with toothpicks. Pour the honey syrup over the cakes and allow it to soak in for a few minutes before serving.

MARCHPANE CAKE

INSPIRED BY **HIS DARK MATERIALS**

His Dark Materials is a fantasy trilogy written by Philip Pullman. Reading His Dark Materials was, for me, very like reading *Peter Pan*, in that it's certainly *about* children but it doesn't seem like it's necessarily *for* children. The story follows a young girl named Lyra, who lives in an alternate universe where people's souls are entities in the form of animals that follow their owners around. The series goes to very unexpected places and although it has very strong fantasy elements, the overall story is a lot more like *Paradise Lost* than *Lord of the Rings*.

Oddly enough, although His Dark Materials (mostly) takes place in an alternate universe, the food is based in reality. There's chocolatl, which is chocolate; Kendal Mint Cakes, which are energy bars used by mountaineers; and blubber, which is, well, marine animal fat. There was one food that stood out and that is the Marchpane (or Marzipan) Cake, which appeared in the third book of the trilogy, *The Amber Spyglass*. I am aware that Marzipan cakes are definitely a real thing, but this one was fairly special. Enjoy with a nice cup of chocolatl; it tastes almost like falling in love . . .

SERVES 8–10

1 Yellow Cake Mix (page 9)
1 tablespoon lemon zest
6 ounces (175 g) almond paste
1½ cups (180 g) almond flour
1½ cups (185 g) confectioner's
  sugar, plus extra for dusting
2 teaspoons almond extract
1 teaspoon rose water
1 egg white
Warmed apricot jelly, for glazing

1 Prepare the Yellow Cake Mix, but in step 2 of that recipe, beat in the lemon zest and almond paste with the butter and sugar. Let the cake cool while you prepare the marzipan.

2 Place the almond flour and confectioner's sugar in a food processor and pulse until combined, making sure you break up any lumps.

3 Add the almond extract and rose water to the food processor and pulse to combine, then add the egg white and process until a thick dough is formed.

4 Dust your work surface with confectioner's sugar, then turn out the almond marzipan dough and knead it a few times.

5 Roll out the marzipan as evenly as possible until it's large enough to cover the cake.

6 Use a clean glazing brush to spread the warmed apricot jelly onto the marzipan. Use your rolling pin to carefully lift the marzipan up and onto the cake, jelly side down. Use your hands to gently press the marzipan onto the cake. The jelly should help with this, acting like glue. Usually it's best to smooth the top first, then the sides. If you notice air bubbles or pleating making things uneven, just lift the marzipan slightly to let the air escape or to unfold the pleat. When the marzipan is smoothly covering the cake, trim the excess from the bottom. Decorate the cake however you like!

ROCK CAKES

INSPIRED BY **HARRY POTTER**

The Harry Potter series is a treasure trove of magical foods and sweets and you may be wondering why you're reading about Rock Cakes right now instead of, say, Pumpkin Pasties or Cauldron Cakes. The truth is, I exhausted a lot of the more universally appealing Harry Potter treats in the first book, so now I have to resort to Hagrid's more questionable cooking.

Right now you may be remembering how Ron nearly chipped a tooth on these cakes and are thinking to yourself, "Maybe I'll just skip this one . . ." but please, hear me out! These are actually really tasty. Hagrid's a half-giant so he may have made these just a bit too hard for the human jaw. I have softened them up a bit (so no, you don't have to book a dental appointment in advance), but they do have a nice crunchy exterior.

MAKES 8–10 CAKES

2 cups (250 g) all-purpose flour
2 teaspoons baking powder
2 teaspoons orange or lemon zest
2 teaspoons Sweet Spice Blend
  (page 12)
1½ cups (3 sticks, or 340 g) unsalted
  butter, chilled
⅓ cup (75 g) packed brown sugar
1½ cups (225 g) dried fruits (raisins,
  currants, cranberries, etc.)
1 egg, beaten
1 teaspoon vanilla extract
1 tablespoon whole milk
Raw cane sugar, for sprinkling

1 Preheat the oven to 350°F (180°C) and line a baking sheet with parchment paper.

2 In a mixing bowl, sift together the flour, baking powder, zest, and spice blend.

3 Cut the butter into small pieces and add to the flour mixture.

4 Use your fingers to rub the butter into the flour mixture until it forms small crumbly pieces. You can do this in a food processor as well, if you have one.

5 Stir in the brown sugar and dried fruit, then add the egg, vanilla, and milk.

6 Spoon 8–10 gobs of the mixture onto the baking sheet, making sure they're spaced out enough for some expanding.

7 Sprinkle the raw sugar liberally over the cakes.

8 Bake for 20–25 minutes, or until a light golden brown color. Serve immediately, if you want them hot.

SEED CAKES

INSPIRED BY **THE HOBBIT**

The Hobbit was Tolkien's precursor to *The Lord of the Rings* trilogy, which is widely accepted as the "grandfather" of high fantasy. Without *The Hobbit*'s success, there may never have been *Lord of the Rings*, which in turn inspired countless other authors to create their own works of fantasy. Without *The Hobbit* and *Lord of the Rings*, we may never have had phenomena like Harry Potter or *Game of Thrones*, or even *Dungeons and Dragons*. Personally, I wouldn't want to live in such a world.

In the beginning of the classic tale, Bilbo very unexpectedly finds his home full of hungry dwarves, and Balin specifically requests seed cakes. Like any respectable Hobbit, Bilbo already had some cakes prepared and is able to serve up these tasty morsels, along with an assortment of other delicious foods, to all thirteen dwarves.

MAKES 12 SMALL CAKES OR 4–5 RAMEKIN CAKES

Cakes

1 Yellow Cake Mix (page 9)
⅛ cup (20 g) caraway seeds
½ cup (70 g) poppy seeds, plus extra for sprinkling
Zest of 1 orange (approximately 1 tablespoon)

Glaze

1½ cups (185 g) confectioner's sugar
¼ cup (60 ml) orange juice, plus more if necessary
1 tablespoon melted butter
½ teaspoon almond extract
1 teaspoon vanilla extract

1 Prepare the Yellow Cake Mix, adding all the seeds and orange zest along with the other dry ingredients in step 4 of that recipe. I recommend using ramekins or muffin tins for baking these cakes.

2 Once the cakes have cooled, carefully remove them from their tins or ramekins.

3 Prepare the glaze. Add the confectioner's sugar to a bowl, then add in the juice, butter, and almond and vanilla extracts. Stir until it forms a smooth glaze. Add more orange juice if it's too thick.

4 Carefully pour the glaze onto the top of each of the cakes and allow it to spread naturally.

5 Once the glaze has spread a bit, sprinkle additional poppy seeds on the tops of the cakes.

PIES AND TARTS

Undertale: **BUTTERSCOTCH CINNAMON PIE**

Twin Peaks: **NORMA'S CHERRY PIE**

Adventure Time: **ROYAL TART**

Alice's Adventures in Wonderland: **QUEEN OF HEARTS' STOLEN TARTS**

The Elder Scrolls V: Skyrim: **SNOWBERRY CROSTATA**

BUTTERSCOTCH CINNAMON PIE

INSPIRED BY **UNDERTALE**

This one comes from a retro-style indie video game called *Undertale*. In *Undertale*, you control a small child who finds themselves in a mysterious and occasionally hostile underground region where nothing is as it seems. *Undertale* is full of surprises and does a great job of turning a lot of video game tropes on their head.

In the beginning of the game, you meet a kind soul named Toriel, who acts as your guide but must leave you for a while. Isn't that just like a video game guide? While you're adventuring by yourself, Toriel calls you on your cell phone and asks whether you prefer cinnamon or butterscotch and you can choose whichever. After spending some time solving puzzles and complimenting frogs, you make your way to Toriel's very cozy home, where she has prepared a butterscotch *and* cinnamon pie for you. This was a fun recipe to create, it's stupid easy and the end result is delicious. Enjoy this pie after a nice spaghetti dinner!

SERVES 6–8

1 Single-Crust Pie Dough (page 8)

Filling
1½ cups (350 ml) whole milk
½ cup (240 g) cream
⅔ cup (150 g) packed light brown sugar
¼ cup (32 g) cornstarch
½ teaspoon salt
½ teaspoon ground cinnamon
2 egg yolks, whisked
1 tablespoon unsalted butter
1 teaspoon vanilla extract

1 Prepare the Single-Crust Pie Dough. Preheat oven to 375°F (190°C).

2 Using a pastry roller, roll out the dough to fit a 9-inch (23 cm) pie tin and press the dough evenly into the bottom and sides of the tin. Cut off any excess.

3 Bake the crust by itself for 7 minutes. Remove from the oven and set aside.

4 Time to start on the filling. In a double boiler, combine the milk, cream, brown sugar, cornstarch, salt, and cinnamon. Stir the mixture using a whisk and keep stirring until it thickens. If you don't have a double boiler, boil water in a saucepan and suspend a stainless steel or Pyrex bowl above, so that no steam can escape. This will heat the contents of the bowl just right, without burning any of it.

Topping

1 cup (120 g) heavy whipping
  cream
2 tablespoons granulated
  sugar
Ground cinnamon,
  for sprinkling

5 Whisk the egg yolks into the mixture, still over the heat, pouring them in slowly. Continue to whisk constantly until the mixture thickens to almost the consistency of pudding. Remove from the heat, then add the butter and vanilla and stir some more, until both are completely incorporated.

6 Pour the mixture into the pie crust. Bake the pie for 7 minutes, then remove from the oven.

7 Let the pie cool for a few minutes on the counter and then transfer it to the fridge until it's at least at room temperature. When it's almost done cooling, prepare the topping. Add the cream and sugar into a mixing bowl and whip with a hand mixer until it forms soft peaks. Be careful not to over-whip.

8 Spread the whipped cream on top of the chilled pie and sprinkle with cinnamon.

NORMA'S CHERRY PIE

It was the mystery of who killed Laura Palmer that captured audiences in the '90s, but *Twin Peaks* has a strange magic that transcends time. One of the many fascinating aspects of *Twin Peaks* was that, despite all of its dark corners, the town remained a place of comfort and familiarity. The insidious evil lurking under the surface didn't make the characters any less lovable, it didn't make the Douglas firs any less majestic, and it certainly didn't make the cherry pie any less delicious.

Everyone knows that the RR Diner—owned and managed by Twin Peak's own former beauty queen, Norma Jennings—is where you go to get a good meal. No doubt everything tastes heavenly at the RR, but there's something miraculous about that cherry pie. Just remember to wash it down with a cup of that damn fine coffee!

SERVES 6–8

- 2 × 14.5-ounce (400 g) cans pitted red cherries
- 1 cup (200 g) granulated sugar
- 3 tablespoons cornstarch
- ¼ teaspoon salt
- ¼ teaspoon almond extract
- 2 teaspoons lemon juice
- 1 tablespoon unsalted butter, softened
- 1 Double-Crust Pie Dough (page 8), rolled and fitted to a 9-inch (23 cm) pie tin
- 1 egg white, for brushing
- Whipped cream, to serve (optional)

1 Preheat the oven to 400°F (200°C).

2 Drain the cherries, reserving ½ cup (120 ml) of the juice. Set aside the cherries and the juice.

3 Combine the dry ingredients—the sugar, cornstarch, and salt—in a mixing bowl.

4 In another mixing bowl, use a spoon to combine the wet ingredients—cherry juice, almond extract, and lemon juice.

5 Add the wet ingredients to the dry ingredients, mixing well. Add the cherries and mix again. Stir in the butter, then let the filling sit for about 15 minutes.

6 Pour the cherry mixture into the pie crust and top with another layer of pie crust, sealing the sides with your fingers. Brush the top of the pie with the egg white, then use a knife to create vents.

7 Bake for 45–55 minutes, or until the crust is golden brown.

8 You can serve the pie warm or let it cool to room temperature before slicing and serving with whipped cream.

ROYAL TART

INSPIRED BY **ADVENTURE TIME**

Oh my glob, a treat from the Land of Ooo! Royal Tarts appeared in the season 2 episode "The Other Tarts." In this episode, Princess Bubblegum tells Jake and Finn that Royal Tarts are the tastiest and most desirable dessert in the Candy Kingdom. The tarts are an essential part of the sacred "Back-Rubbing Ceremony," which requires that only the most perfect tarts be transported to where the illustrious ceremony takes place. However, the journey to relocate the tarts is perilous. Thieves will attempt to steal the tarts, risking their very lives for a taste of Tart glory.

In the episode, the tarts are depicted with a brown tart crust, red on the outside layer, with layers of white and red on the inside, and topped with a berry that looks like a tiny strawberry. Enjoy a slice of perfection with this flaky crust filled with decadent layers of cream and strawberry. It will make you believe that sweetness can win . . . or that you're floating in space? Something mathematical like that.

MAKES 1 TART, 8 SLICES

1 Single-Crust Pie Dough
  (page 8)

Cream

7 egg yolks
1 cup (200 g) sugar
1½ cups (350 ml) scalded milk
3 tablespoons cornstarch
1 teaspoon vanilla extract
1 tablespoon unsalted butter
1 tablespoon heavy cream

1 Fit a 9-inch (23 cm) pie tin with the dough and bake the crust until golden brown, 20 to 25 minutes. Remove from the oven and cool completely.

2 Meanwhile, start on the pastry cream. In a mixing bowl, beat the egg yolks and sugar on medium-high speed for about 5 minutes, or until very thick. Then reduce to low speed and add the cornstarch.

3 With the mixer still on low speed, slowly pour the hot milk into the egg mixture.

4 When all the milk is mixed, pour the cream mixture into a medium saucepan and cook over low heat, stirring constantly with a whisk until the mixture thickens, about 7 minutes. The custard will come together and become very thick, like pudding.

5 Stir in the vanilla, butter, and heavy cream.

Sauce

1 pint (350 g) strawberries
½ cup (100 g) sugar
1 teaspoon vanilla extract
1 teaspoon balsamic vinegar
1 tablespoon water
2 tablespoons cornstarch
Red food dye (optional)

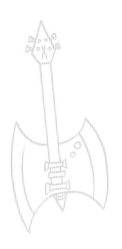

6   Pour the custard through a sieve into a bowl. Cover with plastic wrap and refrigerate until cold.

7   It's time to start the sauce. Set aside a couple of strawberries for garnish. Combine the remaining strawberries, sugar, vanilla extract and balsamic vinegar in a saucepan and bring to simmer over medium heat.

8   Reduce heat to low, cover, and continue to simmer for about 15 minutes.

9   In a small bowl, combine the water and the cornstarch. Whisk this into the simmering saucepan.

10 Cook, stirring constantly, until the mixture thickens, approximately 2 minutes.

11 Remove from the heat. Transfer the mixture to a blender and purée until smooth. You can also use an immersion blender and a bowl if you don't have a stand blender. Add the red food dye, if desired, and stir until the color is evenly dispersed. Refrigerate the sauce until cold.

12 When everything has cooled, spoon the cream into the crust until it's a little less than half full. Make sure it is evenly filled.

13 Add a layer of strawberry sauce on top of the cream and carefully spread it on top of the cream layer. Make sure it is evenly spread.

14 On top of the strawberry sauce, add another layer of cream so that the pie is mostly full. Be careful not to mix the cream and strawberry sauce.

15 Add another layer of strawberry sauce on top of the second cream layer and make sure it is spread evenly and looks good. Be careful not to mix the sauce with the cream.

16 Garnish the tart with the strawberries you set aside and let it cool for another hour to set. Then, enjoy the perfect slice!

QUEEN OF HEARTS' STOLEN TARTS

INSPIRED BY **ALICE'S ADVENTURES IN WONDERLAND**

Alice's Adventures in Wonderland by Lewis Carroll is one of the earliest and most influential fantasy novels. Most of us are familiar with the story: young girl, talking rabbit, tea party, freaky cat, crazy queen with a fondness for beheading, and so on. During Alice's time in Wonderland, she eats some interesting things, including magical cakes, potions, comfits, giant mushrooms, and even pebbles. . . . But there's only one with its very own chapter.

Yup, there is an entire chapter dedicated to the mystery of the Queen's stolen tarts. At the beginning of the chapter, Alice notes a dish of tarts and wishes the court proceedings would end quicker so that she can eat the tasty treats. The entire chapter is a play on an old poem about a knave stealing tarts from a "Queen of Hearts." It is not specifically mentioned what sort of tarts they are, though "pepper" and treacle are suggested by two very clueless characters in Alice. However, I thought jam tarts suited the book more. Jam tarts are a traditional tea-time snack, especially popular amongst children, so it is likely that Alice would be fond of them.

**MAKES 6 LARGE OR
12 SMALL TARTS**

1 Single-Crust Pie Dough (page 8)
½ tablespoon lemon zest
½ tablespoon orange zest
1½ cups (340 g) strawberry jam (or other flavor jam(s) of your choice)

1 Prepare the pie dough, adding the citrus zests along with the dry ingredients in step 1 of that recipe.

2 Roll out the pastry dough about ⅛-inch (3 mm) thick. Cut out a portion of dough to fit your tart tins (heart-shaped or otherwise). Cut off any excess dough and reroll it if needed.

3 Use your fingers to press the dough into the sides and bottom of the tart tins. When all the tins are lined with dough, set aside any excess dough for design.

4 Bake tarts with just the dough inside the tins for 10 minutes and then remove them from oven. Add a few spoonfuls of jam to each tart.

5 Use the excess dough to cut out little heart shapes and place them on top of the jam in the center of each of the tarts.

6 Bake tarts for another 5 minutes, or until crust is golden and jam is settled. Allow the tarts to cool before serving.

SNOWBERRY CROSTATA

INSPIRED BY **THE ELDER SCROLLS V: SKYRIM**

The fifth installment of the *Elder Scrolls* series, *Skyrim*, has had a great legacy, which has been bolstered by the remastered edition released in 2016. There's a lot of food fun to be had in Skyrim, especially with mods that allow you to roll a few thousand cheese wheels down High Hrothgar or fill an entire building with cabbage. And the release includes my personal favorite DLC, Hearthfire.

The primary feature of Hearthfire is that it allows the player to build and customize their own house. It also added several delicious food items to be made in your new custom-built home, like the Snowberry Crostata. Crostatas are one of my favorite desserts to make because they're incredibly simple but they look almost as impressive as seeing a dragon pick up a guard and toss him a few hundred feet in the air. Enjoy with some good old Skyrim snow (vanilla ice cream).

MAKES 1 CROSTATA

1 Single-Crust Pie Dough
  (page 8)
¼ cup (80 g) lemon curd
2 tablespoons all-purpose flour
1 teaspoon vanilla extract
1 teaspoon Sweet Spice Blend
  (page 12)
2 cups (200 g) blueberries
½ tablespoon unsalted butter
1 tablespoon heavy cream
2 tablespoons turbinado sugar

1 Preheat the oven to 425°F (220°C). Line a baking sheet (the kind with sides, in case of leaking) with parchment paper.

2 Roll out the pie dough into a roughly circular shape, about 11 inches (28 cm) in diameter and about ⅛ inch (3 mm) thick. It does not have to be a perfect circle.

3 In a medium mixing bowl, combine the lemon curd, flour, vanilla extract, and spices. Carefully fold in the blueberries. Spoon this mixture over the crust to within 2 inches (5 cm) of the edge.

4 Fold the edge of the crust over the filling, pleating the crust as necessary. Sprinkle the butter over the berries. Lightly brush the crust with the cream, then sprinkle the turbinado sugar on top.

5 Bake for 18–22 minutes, or until the crust is golden brown and the filling is bubbly. Cool for at least 30 minutes before serving.

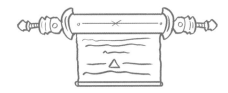

OTHER DESSERTS

Percy Jackson and the Olympians: **BLUE CHOCOLATE CHIP COOKIES**

My Little Pony: Friendship Is Magic: **CHIMICHERRYCHANGA**

Steven Universe: **COOKIE CAT**

Xena: Warrior Princess: **GABRIELLE'S "LITTLE DUMPLINGS WITH THE RED STUFF INSIDE"**

Firefly: **ICE PLANET**

The Big Lebowski: **LINGONBERRY PANCAKES**

The X-Files: **NONFAT TOFUTTI RICE DREAMSICLE**

BLUE CHOCOLATE CHIP COOKIES

INSPIRED BY **PERCY JACKSON AND THE OLYMPIANS**

Percy Jackson and the Olympians follows Percy Jackson, a seemingly normal boy, who has a special heritage as the son of Poseidon. Eventually he meets other demigods and they go on a quest to prevent a war among the gods. I wish this series had been around when I was young because I love Greek mythology, but it is still a super fun read as an adult.

In the first book, *The Lightning Thief*, we find out that Sally, Percy's mother, likes to make blue food. This is because Percy's terrible and smelly stepdad once claimed that blue foods don't exist, and this was Sally's form of rebellion. When Percy has his first drink of Nectar, elixir to the gods that takes on the flavor of the drinker's favorite food, what he tastes is his mom's blue chocolate chip cookies.

MAKES ABOUT 24 COOKIES

1 cup (2 sticks, or 240 g) unsalted
  butter, softened
1 cup (225 g) granulated sugar
1 cup (220 g) packed brown sugar
2 eggs
Blue gel food coloring (or 10 drops
  regular blue food coloring, but the
  cookies will be greener)
2 teaspoons vanilla extract
3 cups (375 g) all-purpose flour
1 teaspoon baking soda
1 teaspoon baking powder
Pinch salt
2 cups (350 g) semisweet
  chocolate chips

1   Preheat the oven to 350°F (180°C).

2   Cream together the butter and both sugars until smooth.

3   Beat in the eggs and gel food coloring, then stir in the vanilla.

4   In a separate bowl, mix together the flour, baking soda, baking powder, and salt.

5   Add the dry ingredients to the wet, stirring until you have a smooth batter, then stir in the chocolate chips. If you want a darker blue, add more dye to the batter when stirring in the chocolate chips.

6   Drop large spoonfuls of the batter onto a parchment-lined cookie sheet. Bake for about 10 minutes.

7   Let the cookies cool and harden a bit before serving, or they'll fall apart, but of course they should still be warm and buttery.

CHIMICHERRYCHANGA

INSPIRED BY MY LITTLE PONY: FRIENDSHIP IS MAGIC

How did a show for little girls become a valid geeky interest for adults? I honestly don't know. Bronies are a strange and fascinating phenomenon. Far and away, I get more requests for *My Little Pony* recipes than from any other fandom. But I'm no neighsayer or parasprite, the love that these geeks have for this show is pure and unquestionable and I respect it immensely. You keep on doing you, bronies! Brohoof!

This little gem of a food concept appeared in the fourteenth episode of the second season called "The Last Roundup." While Applejack is away competing in a rodeo, the ponies receive a letter from Applejack saying she is not planning to return to Ponyville. The ponies immediately track her down to find out what happened, and when Applejack refuses to explain her reasoning, Pinkie Pie is sent to annoy Applejack into fessing up. During Pinkie Pie's relentless rambling, she discusses her idea to make a chimichanga filled with cherries and debates incessantly whether the creations should be called Chimi-Cherries or Cherry-Changas. Luckily, I already have a killer dessert chimichanga recipe in my repertoire, so this is a modified version of that. It tastes pretty much like a churro stuffed with cherry cheesecake. Don't worry, it contains absolutely no oatmeal. . . . That would be crazy.

MAKES 5 CHIMICHERRYCHANGAS

8 ounces (225 g) cream cheese
½ cup (115 g) ricotta cheese
½ cup (115 g) sour cream
1 teaspoon vanilla extract
2 teaspoons lemon zest
Canola or vegetable oil, for
  deep frying
5 large soft flour tortillas
½ cup (100 g) sugar
21 ounces (600 g) cherry filling
Cinnamon sugar, for coating

1 In a large bowl, combine the cream cheese, ricotta, sour cream, vanilla, and lemon zest using a mixer.

2 Heat the oil in your deep fryer or pot to 340°F (170°C). If you do not have a candy thermometer, toss a piece of bread into the hot oil. If it turns golden in about 20 seconds, it's the right temperature. Add the fryer basket now, if you have one.

3 Warm the tortillas in the microwave for a few seconds to soften them. Evenly distribute the cheese mixture amongst the tortillas, spooning it into the center. Do the same with the cherry filling, spooning it on top of the cheese.

4 Tuck in the ends of the tortillas then fold around the filling and roll. If you aren't great with burrito rolling, think of it like wrapping a present, but without tape.

5 Carefully set one of the Cherry-Changas into the hot oil. Fry for about 2 minutes or
   until it is golden brown. If you do not have a fryer basket, use tongs to gently remove
   the Chimi-Cherry from the oil. Roll, brush, or sprinkle it with cinnamon sugar. Repeat
   for each Cherry-Changa. Or Chimi-Cherry. Or Cherry-Changa. Or Chimi-Cherry . . .

COOKIE CAT

INSPIRED BY **STEVEN UNIVERSE**

Steven Universe was created by Rebecca Sugar of *Adventure Time* fame. It centers around the Crystal Gems, a group of extraterrestrial superheroes, and Steven, a half-human boy with powers he's only begun to explore. The series has been praised for its strong characterization and world-building, the latter of which uses elements of both fantasy and sci-fi.

These delicious pets for your tummy appeared in "Gem Glow," the very first episode of the series. In the episode, Steven discovers that Cookie Cats, his favorite ice-cream sandwich, have been discontinued and, unfortunately, that's not the only tragedy Beach City is facing. In the episode, Cookie Cats help Steven to defeat the giant evil eye heading for the town. Cookie Cats might just unlock your crystal powers, or inspire you to burst into song. Possibly both at once! They are so much better than Lion Lickers, which nobody really likes and don't even look like lions.

MAKES 8 COOKIE CATS

Filling

1 pint (475 ml) strawberry and/or
   vanilla ice cream, softened

Cookies

1⅓ cups (165 g) all-purpose flour,
   plus extra for dusting

¼ cup (27 g) unsweetened
   cocoa powder

1 teaspoon baking powder

⅛ teaspoon salt

⅓ cup (80 g) unsalted butter,
   softened

¾ cup (170 g) packed light brown
   sugar

1 tablespoon vanilla extract

2 eggs

1 The first thing you want to do is get a baking sheet that can fit in your freezer, then line it with parchment paper. Spoon and spread your ice cream into an even layer on the baking sheet. If you're using both strawberry and vanilla ice cream, do this in alternating lines. Cover with plastic wrap and freeze overnight.

2 In a mixing bowl, sift the flour, cocoa powder, baking powder, and salt. Set aside.

3 Use a mixer to cream together the butter and brown sugar for about 1 minute or until completely mixed.

4 Turn the mixer to medium-low and add the vanilla extract and the eggs, then beat until the eggs and extract are incorporated, about 1 minute.

continued ▸▸

5   Add the dry flour mixture to the butter mixture. Mix on medium-low for about 1 minute. Everything should be completely incorporated at this point and the dough should be soft and sticky.

6   Lightly dust a work surface with more flour and place the dough on it. Work the dough into about a ½-inch (1 cm) flat circle. Wrap the dough in plastic wrap and refrigerate for at least 1 hour, or until it's firm enough to roll out.

7   Once the dough is firmed up, dust your work surface, the dough, and your rolling pin with flour. Roll out the dough to between ⅛ and ¼ inch (3 and 6 mm) thick.

8   It's actually fairly easy to create the cat shape. Make a template for yourself using paper or cardboard. Draw a wide oval and add two triangular ears on top. Use scissors to cut out the template and place it over the edge of the rolled-out dough. Use a sharp knife to carefully cut the dough around the edges of the template. You can use a soda or water bottle to stamp out the eyes, and you only need to make eye holes for half the cookies.

9   Carefully transfer the cut cookies to a parchment-lined baking sheet. Gather the scraps, work and roll the dough again, then cut out the remaining cookies until you have 16 total. Dust with flour as needed.

10 Place the cut cookies in the refrigerator for 20–30 minutes, which will prevent the cookies from spreading too much and becoming misshapen.

11 Preheat oven to 350°F (180°C) with a baking rack placed in the center. Bake the cookies for 11–12 minutes. They will still feel soft when done, and that's okay. Carefully transfer to a rack to cool completely.

12 Once the cookies are cool and firm, get out your sheet of ice cream. Use the cat template to cut out the cat shape in the ice cream. Place this on top of one of the eyeless cookies, then add one of the cookies with eyes on top. Repeat until all the cookies are used. Chill the completed cookies in your special freezer for at least 20 minutes before serving. They'll keep for about a week.

GABRIELLE'S "LITTLE DUMPLINGS WITH THE RED STUFF INSIDE"

INSPIRED BY XENA: WARRIOR PRINCESS

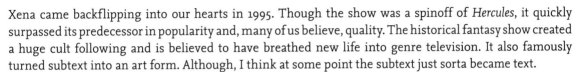

Xena came backflipping into our hearts in 1995. Though the show was a spinoff of *Hercules*, it quickly surpassed its predecessor in popularity and, many of us believe, quality. The historical fantasy show created a huge cult following and is believed to have breathed new life into genre television. It also famously turned subtext into an art form. Although, I think at some point the subtext just sorta became text.

Beautiful women kicking ass and yelling "AHLALALALA!" aside, so much of the show's appeal was the relationship development between Xena and her faithful companion, Gabrielle. This little gem comes from a very endearing moment between the two ladies. In the beginning of the episode "The Furies," Gabrielle challenges Xena to a friendly race. If Gabrielle wins, Xena has to collect all the firewood for one week. If Xena wins, Gabrielle has to make "those little dumplings with the red stuff inside." When Gabrielle seems hesitant to agree, Xena begs, "Oh, please?" So, these things are supposed to be tasty enough to make the warrior princess beg, and they're complicated enough to somehow make Gabrielle unenthusiastic about something for one millisecond. I'd like to think that Gabrielle, clever and resourceful as she is, decided to fill the traditional Greek honey dumpling (*loukoumades*) with red pomegranate preserves, perhaps inventing the first ever jelly donut.

MAKES 16–18 DUMPLINGS

Jelly Filling*

2 cups (475 ml) pomegranate juice

2 tablespoons lemon juice

½ package (1¾ ounces, or 50 g) pectin

1 It's best to make the jelly first. In a small pan over high heat, bring the pomegranate juice, lemon juice, and pectin to a rolling boil, then slowly add the honey.

2 Remove from the heat and skim the foam off the surface. You'll probably have some leftover jelly after filling the dumplings, so if you want to keep it, store it in a sterilized canning jar. Set the jelly aside to cool and jell up.

continued ▶▶

¾ cup (260 g) orange blossom or thyme honey
1 sterilized canning jar

Dough

2 packets (¼ ounce, or 7 g, each) active dry yeast
1 cup (235 ml) water, lukewarm
1 cup (235 ml) whole milk, lukewarm
3 cups (375 g) all-purpose flour
2 tablespoons sugar
2 tablespoons olive oil
Generous pinch salt
Oil, for deep-frying

Toppings

Orange blossom or thyme honey, warmed
Toasted sesame seeds
Ground cinnamon

* Premade pomegranate (or other types of red jellies) are fine here. Pomegranate and quince would be the most historically accurate, not that *Xena*, as a series, had a huge emphasis on historical accuracy.

3   Now, make the dumplings. Dissolve the yeast in the lukewarm water.

4   Using a mixer, mix the remaining dough ingredients except the oil with the lukewarm water until a smooth batter is obtained.

5   Cover and let the batter rise in a warm place until it is around three times its previous size, approximately 45–60 minutes, depending on the temperature and humidity.

6   In a deep fryer or a large heavy bottomed saucepan, heat the oil to about 350°F (180°C). Test that it's hot enough by adding some dough into the hot oil. If the oil immediately bubbles, it is ready.

7   Place a large tablespoon or soupspoon in a glass of lukewarm water near the batter. Scoop about 2 tablespoons dough per puff with the wet spoon, drop it into the wet palm of your hand, and roll it to create a round shape—but do not overwork the dough.

8   Put the dough balls back into the spoon then use the spoon to drop them into the hot oil in batches, wetting the spoon each time you make a dough ball, until there are enough fritters to comfortably fill the surface area of the saucepan without overcrowding.

9   Fry the balls in the hot oil until golden brown on the bottom, then roll them over to cook the other side. When they're finished, gently set the *loukoumades* aside to drain on paper towels.

10   When they're cool enough to handle (but still warm) use a chopstick to poke a hole in the bottom of each ball and rotate the chopstick to clear a space for the jelly.

11   Spoon the jelly into a piping bag fitted with a round tip. Slowly pipe about half a tablespoon of jelly into the center of each dumpling, being careful not to overfill.

12   Drizzle the warm honey onto the finished dumplings then powder with the toasted sesame seeds and cinnamon. Eat up, you just won a race!

ICE PLANET

INSPIRED BY **FIREFLY**

Of all the problematic fictional foods, this is the most problematic. This playful abomination appeared in the beginning of "The Message," while the gang is on an excursion to a bazaar of some kind. Much like a viewing booth for a mutated cow fetus, this overly elaborate treat is clearly just a way for the street vendors to swindle visitors out of their hard-earned bits.

Because this is a problematic novelty food, this recipe is much more crafts project than food recipe. You can use any kind of ice cream you want and roll it in whatever "toppings" you like, but if you're looking to get the same color as River's Ice Planet, I suggest using white-colored ingredients like vanilla ice cream, nuts, yogurt chips, or white chocolate. But, keep in mind, it don't matter if you're some kind of mind-reading genius, you'd better be up for getting hit in the face with a ball of ice cream.

SERVES 2–4

"Planet"

½ cup (75 g) macadamia nuts, chilled

½ cup (60 g) white chocolate chips, chilled

3–4 scoops vanilla ice cream

Supplies

Powder-free vinyl gloves

Straw

Scissors

Parchment paper

White twine

12-inch (30 cm) wooden dowel (the kind typically used for cake rods)

Scotch tape

Paper star cutouts

1 Use a blender or food processor to crumble the nuts and white chocolate, if they are not already a small size. Don't overdo it and melt the chocolate, or it will clump. Set the crumbles in a wide bowl.

2 Put on the gloves and use your hands to gather the ice cream around the straw. When you have a rough ball of ice cream sticking around the straw, transfer it to the bowl of crumbled nuts and white chocolate, coat the ball with them and use the bowl to help roll a more perfect round shape.

3 Snip off the ends of the straw with the scissors so they do not show. Place the ball of ice cream on a plate or a tray of some sort, lined with parchment paper, and freeze it for a couple of hours, until it's fairly solid.

4 Tie the twine around the wooden dowel, so you have a fishing rod situation going on. You may need to carve out a notch in the dowel so that the twine doesn't slide off. Use scissors to snip the twine so there's about 12 inches (30 cm) hanging from the dowel.

5 Take the planet with the straw in the center and lower the string into the straw until it comes out the other side. Tie a knot in the string so that when you lift the dowel the planet will be secured by the knot and not slide off. You may need to tie it multiple times to make a knot thick enough to not go through the straw.

6 Cut three small pieces of Scotch tape and stick them to various points on the string. Pinch them so they go completely around the twine but still have flaps from which to stick your pretty star cutouts.

7 Once you've added the stars, your Ice Planet is ready for your futile attempts to eat it.

LINGONBERRY PANCAKES

INSPIRED BY **THE BIG LEBOWSKI**

The Big Lebowski is easily the most quoted Coen Brothers' film. It stars Jeff Bridges, who many of us geeks will remember as the guy from *Tron*, but many more folks know him as The Dude. The Dude's adventures begin when his home is invaded by a couple of thugs who've mistaken him for someone else: a wealthy man who shares his name, Jeffrey Lebowski. The Dude decides to visit this other Lebowski and demand he pay for the damages to his apartment, particularly his defiled rug. That's when things go wrong.

Lingonberry Pancakes appeared in a scene towards the end of the film. You may recall the scene as the one that made you go "OMG is that Aimee Mann and Flea?!" While in a diner, the German Nihilists all order Lingonberry Pancakes, except for Flea, who orders "Pigs in Blanket." Actually, Aimee Mann orders "Heidelbeerpfannkuchen," which is blueberry pancakes in German, but it is incorrectly translated to Lingonberry Pancakes by her boyfriend. Wash these delicious babies down with a White Russian* . . . unless you don't like White Russians, then, well, The Dude does not abide.

* For those who don't know, a "White Russian" is vodka, coffee liqueur, and cream, typically at a 5:2:3 ratio.

MAKES 15 PANCAKES

2 eggs
2 cups (475 ml) milk
1¼ cups (155 g) all-purpose flour
¼ cup (50 g) granulated sugar
Pinch salt
¼ cup (½ stick, or 60 g) unsalted
  butter, melted
Vegetable oil or butter, for frying
Lingonberry preserves, to taste
Confectioner's sugar, to serve
Whipped cream, to serve

1 Beat the eggs in a medium bowl until foamy. Add the milk, flour, sugar, and salt, stirring until fully mixed. Lastly, stir in the melted butter.

2 Cover the batter with plastic wrap and refrigerate for at least 2 hours, but overnight is better.

3 Heat some vegetable oil or butter over medium-high heat in a skillet or griddle. Pour a thin stream of batter into a circular shape onto the hot griddle or skillet, keeping in mind that the pancakes should be 5–6 inches (13–15 cm) in diameter and very thin. Cook the pancake on one side for 20 seconds, flip, and cook on the other side for 20 seconds until done. Set the cooked pancake aside and repeat until you have about 15 pancakes, adding more oil or butter as needed to prevent sticking.

4 Spread the lingonberry preserves in the center of a pancake, then roll the pancake up around the preserves so they're tube-shaped. Repeat for each pancake.

5 Sprinkle the completed pancakes with powdered sugar and top with whipped cream.

 KITCHEN NERD NOTES

Lingonberry jelly may be a little hard to find at a grocery store, but it'll definitely be at your local Ikea or online.

NONFAT TOFUTTI RICE DREAMSICLE

INSPIRED BY **THE X-FILES**

The X-Files dominated the '90s geek scene. It somehow made extraterrestrial conspiracy theories cool. The dynamic between believer Mulder and skeptical Scully is now the stuff of legends. During their search for the truth, there have been some rare food moments. Like that one time when Scully was somehow still dignified and sexy with a face covered in barbecue sauce and stuffing ribs into her mouth. One of the many reasons Scully is my hero.

This little gem appears in a delightful scene from the Season 6 episode, "The Unnatural," in which Mulder teases Scully about her frozen dessert and life choices. So, we have some clues about what's going on with this "ice cream" abomination: there's tofu, rice, and orange-vanilla flavor served in a cone. Unfortunately, it's impossible to make this truly "nonfat." I've never seen non-fat tofu. Despite this, or probably because of it, the recipe actually results in some pretty tasty vegan ice cream. This is just speculation, but I'm pretty sure that, despite his assertions otherwise, it tastes significantly better than the air in Mulder's mouth, though I'm sure some of us wouldn't mind testing that particular theory!

MAKES A QUART OF "ICE CREAM"

Equipment
Ice cream maker

"Ice Cream"
16 ounces (450 g) silken tofu
2¼ cups (540 ml) vanilla rice milk
¼ cup (90 g) agave nectar, or more
1 teaspoon orange extract
½ teaspoon vanilla extract
1½ teaspoons xanthan gum
Sugar waffle cones, to serve

1 Blend all the ingredients except for the xanthan gum and waffle cones in a blender.

2 While the blender is blending, slowly sprinkle in the xanthan gum.

3 When the base is smooth and creamy, pour into a container and place in the fridge until the ingredients are cold—about 2 hours (this timing depends on your fridge, the initial temperature of the ingredients, and so on).

4 Use the base according to your ice cream maker's instructions.

5 Freeze for 30 minutes before scooping into the waffle cone.

INDEX

ACKNOWLEDGMENTS

My mom, Rolanda Conversino, thank you for all the pre-editing editing. Also, thank you for buying all the supplies for Pie Day 2016, helping prep all the pies, and even bravely volunteering to taste-test the herring pie when no one else would. Also, big thanks to Joe Conversino, who let me mess up his kitchen again and even had to clean it up this time.

My big brother, Nicholas Reeder, for his help editing, cooking, and testing. Also, thank you for kindling my love for cooking and always being there for me, in both culinary and non-culinary crises.

Thanks to Denis Caron of Corvink Co. for creating the amazing illustrations for both cookbooks!

Jessica and Wesley Garcia, you guys took on a lot of testing again, and I am forever grateful. Can't wait to have you guys over for midnight margaritas, fort-building, and Aladdin!

My beautiful cousin, Ashley Finley, Thankee-sai for taking on Gunslinger Burritos and Jawa Juice! May Ka, the Force, and my love, be with you.

Amanda, Brian, and Beowulf Backur, thank you for your support and input, so proud to call you guys family.

Lesley Daus, thanks for taking on two of the most beastly recipes in their class . . . and for bringing my sister from another mister, Cassandra Rabini, into this world.

Seonaid Uebelheardt, I have many reasons to be thankful to you, your help testing Ambrosia is just one of many. And thanks to Seonaid's lovely daughter, Ali Nakata, for volunteering to test Flaming Fire Flakes—I have a feeling we'd be great friends.

Terry Daus, thank you for preventing the dry mushroom apocalypse!

Thanks to my husband for tending to the things I didn't have time or energy to tend to while writing this cookbook and incubating human life. My neuropathways have become quite accustomed to your sensory input.

Thanks to Jay Perez for his sage wisdom on '90s anime.

My boss, Lara Bonaquisiti, and my lovely team at my day job, Dani Alvarez, Trianna Testoni, and Tracy Urban, who have been so supportive of my extracurricular activities.

Finally, thank you to all the people at Quarto, past and present, who helped make the first book a success and let me make another one!

ABOUT THE AUTHOR

Cassandra Reeder is an author, avid home cook, and lifetime geek. For almost a decade, she has been helping other geeks and nerds all over the world make their fictional food fantasies come true at www.geekychef.com. In 2014, she released *The Geeky Chef Cookbook*, which, to her immense delight and gratitude, has been very well received. Cassandra currently lives in Portland, Oregon, with her husband and pet parrot, and there's a little geek-in-training expected to beam in very soon.

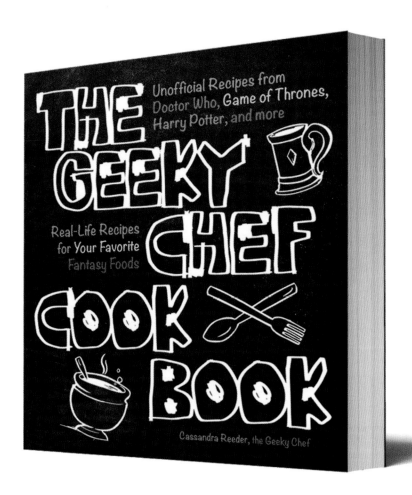

SOMETHING MISSING?

While browsing through this book, you might be saying to yourself, "*What kind of honorless pataq leaves out Gagh?*" or "*One does not simply forget Lembas,*" or maybe "*What about the Turkish Delight? Think of the children!*" Don't panic! If it seems obvious and it's missing, it's probably in the first *The Geeky Chef Cookbook*. Be sure to pick up a copy!